THE

BUTCHER'S

DAUGHTER

For Seth
In memory of your grandparents, Aaron and Helen
And in memory of Joe

Try to look. Just try and see.

Charlotte Delbo *Auschwitz and After*

I

Outside, America Waits

Nobody's Business

Were they in concentration camps?" a high school friend asks upon learning my parents are European Jews.

"They survived in the Polish woods," I say, steering the conversation elsewhere.

Mameh, hearing German rifle shots, crouched low in a snowy trench, next to two quivering deer.

Tateh ran, without his first wife and children.

To bury their dead, they dug graves using spoons.

In my home, framed photos of dead relatives stared out from our walls. Images of the martyred many spilled over from albums and shoe-boxes, apparitions rising into the ether like ghosts.

I was raised with them, the slain, the lost.

It's nobody's business.

Immigrant/1951

I remember a bitter taste and the color gray; the gray of water and wave, the rock gray of wall, floor and railing, the silvery gray sparkle of flying fish, their splash of tail and fin accompanying us on our journey across the Atlantic.

Mameh coaxes orange sections to settle my stomach. Juice dribbling from the corners of my mouth, I'm nestled against her, twirling my hair, back and forth, back and forth in rhythm to the up and down shifting of the big ship. We're on the USNS General Harry Taylor, a Navy transport now freighted with refugees. Leaving Heidelberg, from Bremerhaven, ten days rocking and tumbling across ocean. Ten days pressed against each other amid the wailing of babies, amid the chatter of Yiddish, Polish and German, the barking of English, and the dazed gaze of the stateless immigrants animated only by the excited call of *kik, kik*—"look, look," at the first sighting of land.

At the Port of New York we disembark into a cavernous room whose harsh light makes me squint. People mill about lugging suitcases, some bound in old twine.

Families huddle together on great wooden benches and in small clusters under windows spanning floor to ceiling. Trunks are piled like blocks in empty corners. A uniformed man approaches carrying a clipboard, asking Tateh and Mameh questions in a language none of us understand. Mameh contracts, head lowered, eyes fastened on the shiny lower buttons of his jacket. Tateh clears his throat, rearranges his shoulders to expand his bulky frame and offers papers. The man stamps them, pins a tag on my coat bearing my name and number. I clutch Gerda, my doll, grip Mameh's hand tight.

Outside, America waits.

My Brother is Born an American

The woman runs her palm around her swollen belly and grunts. Already she hates this thing growing inside her, this thing she can't control. Already she feels its greed, taking, taking until she has not a hair left to give. She can hardly look at me, the one she has now, born soon after the war. The woods, the nightly fires, her uncle's blood; she still smells it all. She took the memories into her entire body then, of her father, brother, uncle, and now there is no room for more. But each day now brings an intrusion into the gauzy curtain she's drawn between herself and the outside. The woman wants only to sit immobile behind that curtain and be absorbed by nothing. "Nothing" is safe, "nothing" is home, "nothing" is no memory. Children insist on pulling that curtain away, wanting to be fed, clothed, talked to, held. The woman has so far endured the motions, attending to childcare with fast, hard movements, always eager to return to her own nothing.

This new one, she knows, will be strong, insistent,

and so, one afternoon, when her belly is almost ready to burst, she climbs onto the kitchen table, pulls her hands into tight fists by her sides, closes her eyes and jumps. Landing crumpled on the floor, she feels a rush of warm liquid between her legs, the sharp twisting of her insides, and she begins to scream, loud, piercing cries.

The beast rouses to sharpen its claws on the corner wall, then, circling the floor, grunts and snakes into a curl.

Much later, in the hospital with her husband by her side, the nurse brings a child to her. Wrapped in a blue blanket, its body smells of damp earth and talcum. The woman, refusing to look, turns her face to the wall, and says,

"This is not mine. I had a dead baby. Take it away."

The husband, not knowing how to respond to this stranger, his wife, begins to laugh. The nurse hesitates a moment, puts the child between them, then quietly leaves the room.

And that is how my brother came into the world.

I Feel Myself Dissolving

Twirling thumb and index finger through a lock of brown hair, I caress the soft smooth strands draping my neck. Back and forth, back and forth, like silk against skin. A habit I'm told acquired in infancy at Mameh's breast, it recalls milk and warmth and the comfort of adults. A habit I carried onto the USNS General Harry Taylor, it soothed me as the big ship tumbled across ocean while waves crashed against railings, fish frolicked on the water's surface, and nausea, a tightness in my throat, lasted days. It was a habit I used to soothe myself then, one that transports me into sleep, into forgetting, at least for the night, Mameh's angry words.

Mameh riles often these days.

This time, I made noise and woke my brother.

I haven't discovered yet that Mameh wonders why she's still alive, still gets up each morning tasting bitterness, choking on air, while the men in her family, her brother, father, uncle are all dead. I haven't discovered yet that Mameh views her own womanhood as less than:

less than men, less than intelligent, less than worthy. For now I'm convinced I must be bad if Mameh says so.

I stroke a lock of hair, back and forth, between thumb and index finger, back and forth, rocking gently and wondering when my mother will return. She's been gone for what seems hours.

"Shopping," she had said.

I watch my little brother sleeping. He's moving his legs around in circles, as though already practicing to walk away, occasionally hitting ankle or toe against the side of his crib. How would it feel to pick him up, carry him over to the window, open it and let go? I've heard that a penny dropped from the top of the Empire State Building can gather so much speed and strength that, like a bullet, it can kill a person on impact. I imagine my brother, crimson pajamas somersaulting down five stories, picking up speed, a red baby bullet.

Sometimes my body feels far away from me, like the echo of an El train after it disappears from rails. I've been twirling my hair continuously since my brother was born, fingering, holding on, needing this contact with my body, to prove this body is solid flesh and bone that can be touched, felt.

Hearing the familiar rattle of key against lock I rush to the door, eager to greet my mother, eager to show her my own eagerness. Mameh's face is flushed from the summer's heat, beads of sweat blossoming on her forehead from the sticky Bronx air. Her cotton dress clings to her, half moons formed under her arms. She lays her packages on top of the kitchen table, absent-mindedly pushing aside the candelabra she'll light for tonight's *Shabbos*. She keeps one bag with her as she walks towards the crib, a white bag decorated with greens, reds, blues and yellows streaming like confetti alongside the edge and crease of paper. My brother, awake now, coos as he extends his arms up to her, wanting to be lifted out, to crawl around the apartment floor. My mother smiles and raises him high over the slats, letting out a grand *Oompah* as she releases him onto the black and white checked linoleum floor. He curls himself head to toe, peers up at her sideways as she reaches into the bag and pulls out a soft plush puppy, its pink tongue lolling in a goofy doggie smile, its plastic eyes rounded, like my brother's, in doggie delight.

Gnawing on the Bone of Belonging

The neighborhood strays, mongrel pack dogs, weave in and out of traffic, their muscle, fur and sinew loping alongside steel. I imagine these exotic creatures to have emerged from some wild, lush place. Traveling together, seeming to possess the rambling streets, they form a rich mass of tan, gray and black patches.

In silence, I follow, pretending to be one of them.

Here, on the streets, or in Crotona Park, I'm away from my parents' arguing, my brothers cries, from the stifling atmosphere of *that thing* I don't yet understand, its weight seeping into the very walls of our home.

Mameh calls it *Dee Melchome*.

The Weight of Hidden Words

When I speak, the other children in my third grade class lean over their desks, straining to hear.

"A weak voice," Mrs. Hamilton says.

I can barely speak above a whisper. Sometimes my mouth forms words that seem to come from outside my body, as though fished from the air swirling around me and not from inside myself. Sometimes I think hard about the words before speaking, then they stumble around my tongue, racing and crawling all at once.

I stutter.

"Speak up," the teacher urges.

I hoard my words. Like Oreo cookies, I don't want to use them up.

I believe each of us is allotted a finite number of words per lifetime, these words housed in invisible satchels held deep within ourselves. Kings or queens are allotted extra bags containing foreign words used in emergencies, or diplomatic matters, such as meetings to end wars.

"Sally sells sea shells by the sea shore," Mrs. Smith, the speech teacher, says, "Repeat."

Every Thursday and Friday Sally opens shop to do business, which I then pronounce, syllable by syllable. My words tumble out in a whisper.

"Louder," Mrs. Smith demands sitting across from me in the dusty Bronx schoolroom.

Stubborn sounds rustle softly like breeze through dunes. I imagine Sally and Peter-the-Pickled-Pepper-Picker sitting underneath the boardwalk, sipping orange soda, passing popcorn, enunciating together, *sibilant*.

Ward and I are the only two white children in Mrs. Hamilton's class. Ward, who is fatherless, has blue eyes, blond hair and a blind mother he helps get around. I have a crush on Ward who wears thick glasses. One day Ward asks to come to my house to play.

"Only Jews here," Mameh says after I ask her.

"Unfair," I want to shout, but keep quiet instead.

Quiet is better. Better than shouting. Better than the buzzing beginning to swell inside my head. Quiet is better than upsetting Mameh.

I didn't know then that in Poland, where Mameh came from, Jewish children were commonly taunted, beaten and cursed by their Christian counterparts. I didn't realize she may be have been protecting me.

I next come across Ward on the street, his arm threaded through his mother's elbow, guiding her tap-tapping across a busy street. He's hunched close to her, looking right and left, walking slowly, with care, as others rush by. They walk in lockstep, as one, Ward's vigilance noble to my eyes.

Turning, I walk the other way.

Like Witches Maybe

In Poland I vas guerrilla, Tateh told me.

In my child's mind, I was perplexed.

I had seen gorillas in picture books.

Although big like a gorilla, my father didn't look like one. For one thing, he lacked fur.

Perhaps he lost his thick coat in Poland.

Or maybe a witch transformed him, back then, in the woods.

That must be it, I reasoned. I knew something bad had happened in the woods to Tateh and Mameh.

Something evil.

Like witches maybe.

Dee Melchomeh, Out from Shadow

The warm glow behind barred windows beckons me on this drizzly November evening toward the single lit building on the block, the library, a beacon in a sea of iron-kettle black. Warehouses flank the building, rising as dark stone, impenetrable. The street markets, closed and gated, boast sidewalk dumpsters, sole reminders of the days' activities.

During the day a constant swell of people crowd the markets, their paper packages brimming over as they scurry from one shop to another. A steady drone drifts through the streets. Children's voices, mingling with their parents chatter, add to the hum and horn of cars, the bickering of chickens. Occasionally frantic shrieks pierce the air. Once from a woman bolting down the street, her blouse torn, right breast exposed, blood blooming on white fabric.

"Stabbed," someone said.

I quicken my pace along damp streets and smell the dumpsters before I see them. The air carries the sharpness of bits of fish, the ink and flesh of newspapers stained with scales that sparkle in the diminished light; rotten fruit, sweet and dying; and chicken feathers, pungent with the odor of new slaughter. Two men walk by and look at me in a way I know to be the wrong way for grown men to look at a nine-year-old. With a quick glance over my shoulder, I hurry into the library. My limbs relax, my breath tapers as I cross its threshold. It's Thursday night, the late night, and I am in my refuge.

Tonight I can take my time scouring the shelves of books, deciding which ones to bring to Miss Chisholm, the librarian, and check out this week. But first, I pass the card catalogue, head for a familiar section and reach for my old friend, *The Brothers Grimm Fairy Tales*. I feel its heft as I carry it over to the table, the red and gilt jacket elegant to my eyes. Riffling through the pages, I enjoy the smooth feel of paper as it floats through my fingers. I let my eyes wander over letters, back and forth, unfocused at first. Black forms against white invite me to look, no, to go in between the spaces and inhabit another world. I linger over the illustrations. The line and color on the page affirms what I see in my mind's eye, giving it beauty and form. Here a barefoot Snow White sits up in bed, awakened by the dwarfs surrounding her. She sees them for the first time. The dwarfs' red and yellow caps flop over their ears, their long white beards curl at the tips. Their future unknown, in this moment there is only possibility. Here too are changeling frogs turned into handsome princes; ragged kitchen maids miraculously dressed in gold, silver and silk, dancing through the night at fancy balls; children outsmarting cannibalistic witches. Here magic and terror coexist. Turning to *Hansel and Gretel*, I begin to read.

I believe in magic, not the yanking a white rabbit out of a top hat kind, but the magic of my own fairy godmother, a luminous specter in flowing white who often stands at the foot of my bed, smiling. The embrace of her smile holds the real magic for me. She bears a striking resemblance to Glinda, the Good Witch of the North, who glides gently among her subjects, her voice ringing like tiny bells. Like Glinda, my fairy godmother has blond curls cascading down her shoulders, and although she never speaks to me, I am certain her voice bears that same musical high pitch. She is as real to me as the chewed-up gum I layer under my bed, and then finger to calm myself.

My room is simple, a three-drawer dresser against one wall, a closet, and my bed, which abuts the window. On top of the dresser, my library books share space with Timothy, a small painted turtle, a Woolworth's purchase, who inhabits his own plastic island. Long forgotten dolls, limbs askew, are piled together in one corner of my closet. My Lincoln Log set is within easy reach in the closet's center, windows and doors carefully packed in cellophane, brown logs arranged according to size. I often construct my own house, live in it for a time.

My fairy godmother appears for the first time the night that Tateh cries. That night begins just like any other. As usual, Tateh returns home around seven-thirty p.m., exhaustion lining his face after a day at the meat-packing factory, an hour's subway ride away. Random cuts scatter across his hands, crisscrossing his fingers and palm. A cloth bandage covers his right thumb, the result of another slip of his sharp knife. Tateh often complains bitterly about the factory, has been saving money to buy his own butcher shop. I picture him, standing at his station, alongside men speaking languages he doesn't understand, quietly working his knives: chopping, trimming, cutting. Busy with his own dream.

With a loud sigh, Tateh seats himself at the kitchen table, removes shoes and socks and waits, while Mameh reaches under the sink for the plastic basin and fills it with warm water and Epsom Salts. The ritual of soaking, a daily restorative to his yellowed, cracked toenails, coarse feet and bruised soul. Mameh returns to the stove, her back to Tateh. Enveloped in steam rising from the pots, she stirs mechanically, seemingly lost in thought. The odors of chicken, potatoes and canned peas mingle and permeate our small apartment, temporarily cloaking the more permanent odor, a mixture of cabbage, cigarettes, and roach spray.

Perhaps it began with a look or a wrong word.

In seconds the air filled with venom, the bellow of their voices mounting to shrieks. I imagine their sharp words slicing through the brick of our building and each one, like a razor edged top, spinning out of control. I imagine *Dee Melchomeh* has crept out from shadow and, like an evil spirit, invaded their bodies. Tateh rises, standing bug-eyed and barefoot in a lukewarm pool of salty water, crimson faced. Mameh, shutting the cook top in one sweeping gesture, turns sharply to face him, nostrils flaring, waving her spoon like a weapon.

In Yiddish Mameh hisses,

"A death to you!"

Does she think of her father, who died in the crematoria of Majdanek, when she screams,

"You should be consumed by fire!"

And from Tateh, is he thinking of his sister or his parents, when he shouts back,

"You should be slaughtered!"

They take no notice of me as I disappear under the kitchen table in time to avoid plates flying across the room, crashing in great chunks to the floor. The table stands flush against the wall. The oilcloth covering forms a veil in front of me. I can peek out and see them if I want to but right now I want more than anything to be elsewhere.

My parents are in another place. Maybe they'll never come back to quiet. Covering my ears with my hands, I bend over my knees, shut my eyes tight and try to remember whom I played with at recess that day. I wait for a lull, and then, as I've been taught at school fire drills, as quietly and quickly as I could, head for my room. Crossing its threshold, I turn on a light, reach for a book and close my bedroom door.

Eventually they exhaust themselves and the apartment is hushed. I hear Tateh announce he's heading to the *schvitz*, and Mameh threaten to replace the apartment lock as he slams the door behind him. Tateh often retreats to the *schvitz*, the steam baths on the Lower East side, to cool down. It must remind him of Glusk, his Polish village, before all the Jews vanished: to ghetto, or forest, or death camp. I imagine him in that windowless chamber, swathed in towels, seated on a pine-slatted bench after a *pletzal* scrub, his back still raw from the oak branches. Engulfed in a cloud of steam, I see him gossip and play cards with the other men, the damp cards curling at the edges. Moisture seeps from the ancient gray tiles, an urban rainforest, covering everyone, everything. Drenched, I imagine he laughs with pleasure at the telling of his own jokes. Here the only arguing is over gin rummy, easily resolved with an exchange of nickels and dimes, the only complaint, someone grumbling about the heat. Later on he'll nap on one of the dorm style cots, then strengthen himself with *schnapps* and smoked fish before returning home. Sometimes he's there all night.

Mameh, sweeping up the broken pieces, mutters curses to herself as she bends low over the dustbin. I know to stay out of her way. Accustomed to these volcanic outbursts I understand the surface explosions to be just that, surface. The rock and molten lava of *Dee Melchomeh*, The War, forms the subterranean, dangerous foundation in each of my parents.

It's one of the first words I hear as a child. My parents frequently use words like *Antesemmit* and *Dee Melchomeh*, and other words I don't understand. They hiss and growl as they form in my parents' mouths. I know these are grim words, not for discussion. I also know these are not concrete every day things like lollipops or light bulbs, or potentially dangerous in the way of roving gangs or cars, though dangerous they are. When I hear my parents utter *Dee Melchomeh*, their voices rise, their eyes widen as though the words surprise them still. *Dee Melchomeh*, our resident underground monster, lies heavy and solid beneath every corner of our thoughts and actions. Late at night he surprises us by lunging into our dreams, often causing my parents to cry out in sleep. Aroused he breathes fire that rushes through my parents and explodes outward in great bursts of anger. Tonight, spent, he coils back into shadow.

"*Feigeleh, schlufts nokh?*"

I am awakened by the urgency of Tateh's question.

Yes, I'm sleeping. It's the middle of the night, I think.

Pulling my blanket up to my chin I surface to his voice. Opening my eyes I can barely recognize his form in the darkness. His face is close to mine. His breath smells odd. He's crying, his sobs, deep and low pitched are so different from my own. It scares me. I don't want to hear him cry. Tateh, the man of the house, needs to be strong to protect me. He needs to shield me from the Nazis who might storm into the house at any moment. Tateh is crying. I am on my own.

And then, in between sobs, in Yiddish,

"Your Mameh doesn't love me, you're the only one who loves me."

I reach under the bed to finger my gum. This time the familiar bumps and grooves feel only like stale gum, nothing more. I close my eyes and hold my breath.

I soon hear him leave the room.

Half-formed questions swirl inside my head, questions that I only fully understood much later, that haunt me for years. What does Tateh want from me? Am I, as a daughter, expected to love Tateh, as Mameh apparently does not? Does he expect me to heal him? To replace my missing sisters from his first family? It's a job I do not want. Is it safe to love him at all, this brute of a man who is just as likely to cry as he is to rage?

I toss, punch my pillow, gradually fall into a sleep so shallow I become aware of a slight rattling at my window, a rustling sound at the foot of my bed. I turn to see her bathed in an aura of half-light, regal, an angel dressed in softest white. My fairy godmother. Her smile is gentle as a caress, her arms outstretched like wings. I'm wrapped in silky warmth and imagine living there forever, in her smile, in her arms, as I drift into deep, delicious sleep.

"You're checking this out again?" Miss Chisholm asks as I hand her *The Brothers Grimm Fairy Tales*, the last of my pile.

"If I'm not mistaken that's the third time in a row," she continues taking her glasses off her nose, letting them dangle from their chain.

"It's for a book report," I fib.

"Well, enjoy it," she says.

Miss Chisholm gets up to remind the remaining stragglers that the library is closing for the evening.

Outside, fog curls around the yellow head of a lamppost and rises. I hear footsteps behind me, clunky and uneven, and turn to see an old woman, wearing a knobbed coat, whose heavy brown stockings are wrinkled around her ankles. She's walking slowly, with a cane. Behind her, the same two men I saw earlier. I hurry to turn the corner and head for home.

The Dead Have Something to Say

The first thing I notice is the icy steel table, just wide enough to hold her body. The room smells faintly of disinfectant. Glass bottles filled with a variety of colored liquids line shelves along the wall. Surgical instruments and gauze lie casually displayed near the stainless steel sink. The funeral director has left a note for me. Her Hebrew name is *Bracha Bat Yitzhak v'Sara*. Bracha, daughter of Isaac and Sarah. She is a fellow synagogue congregant, someone I had not known. I say a quick prayer, adding the traditional "Forgive me Bracha if I do anything to offend you." The harsh fluorescent light sharpens the contours of her body wrapped beneath a thin white sheet. I want to look at her, but hesitate, afraid to remove the flimsy barrier between us.

I grew up with the dead. Framed photographs of the dead lined our bedroom walls. In drawers, uneven stacks of photos spilled out of lopsided shoeboxes, becoming sacred objects that were kept and wept over. Death became something to play with.

Summers at Orchard Beach, the Riviera of the South Bronx, I swam out from shore, away from the fathers' garrulous card games, the mothers' incessant reproaches to the children, away too from the mournful twang of Yossel's battered mandolin. Muscles slack, I floated on my back, savored the gentle push and rock of waves, the soft blanket of water enveloping me. Then I'd lay face down, arms outstretched, empty my mind, and squeeze air from my lungs until they burned.

One evening I decided to become a corpse. I don't recall why, perhaps one of my parents said or did something that wounded me. I lay atop my bed, eyes closed, barely breathing, still as stone. Wrapped in this darkness of my own choosing, I waited. My brother, unable to rouse me, called Mameh, then Tateh, whose increasingly panicked voice prompted me to open my eyes. I wanted to see what all the fuss was about. I wanted to be kept and wept over. Dead would surely get notice.

I learned about them through the photographs. Sweet-faced Nissan, Mameh's youngest brother, who stared out at the camera with the smooth certainty of youth. His body, buried in the Lublin rubble of German bombs, never found. Zayde Duvid, my grandfather, whose long white beard and fierce expression sometimes made me glad not to have known him. Captured in the woods along with his brother, Fetter Nussan, on the

34

third night of Hanukkah, Mameh last saw him wrapped in a *tallis*, a prayer shawl, before she ran deeper into the forest.

There were no photos of my half-sisters, Chava and Rivka, other than one I held in my imagination. I knew of them, knew they were swept up in the whirlwind. Tateh never spoke of them. With my careful prodding, pieces of their story emerged slowly over the years. Along with their mother they were likely shot in transit from the Lublin Ghetto to Piasek.

I pictured them in a lush garden, alongside a pebbled fountain. Chava, who liked to sing, smiled widely from beside our father's long legs, while young Rivka, braids tied in ribbons, rode high up in his arms clutching the back of his neck. Crossing barriers of time and place, we played together and shared secrets. They told me about Poland and the hillside near the flour mill where pale blue flowers blossomed in summer, and about their favorite hiding places along the river. I described our small Bronx apartment and whispered about our father, who screamed in his sleep sometimes. They never told me about leaving for Piasek.

I called them Chava and Rivka. By the time I asked their true names, sometime after Tateh died, no one could recall.

There were many others. Sepia colored frayed photographs of aunts, uncles, grandparents, cousins, staring wide-eyed. *Remember me, don't ever forget,* the beloved, martyred dead whispered into every corner of my soul. I often dreamt of them, countless numbers in rags, surrounding me, a rootless chorus, demanding to be let in, to claim a space to call home. They took up so much room. God, how I hated them.

Reluctant suddenly to face death, I am about to perform, for the first time, *tahara,* an ancient ritual of purifying and dressing Bracha, readying her to stand before God one final time. I regret having responded so quickly to a call for volunteers for new members of the *Hevreh Kadisha,* the burial society. At the time I thought I was uniquely qualified to minister to the dead, but now I'm not so sure. Holding my breath, I remove the sheet and look. Here is a thin, eighty-something woman, her skin the color of wheat flour, fine white hair framing the delicate features of her face. Her face is devoid of expression. The map of her body carries the edges, creases, and folds of a long life, the hard and soft of mother, daughter, wife and friend. Filling several pitchers with lukewarm water I begin the purification. Pouring water over her seven times I recite:

A fountain for gardens. A well of living waters and flowing streams. And Shechina will have washed away the sins of the daughters of Zion, and have purified the blood of Jerusalem with a searing breath. And I will pour upon you pure water and you will be purified...

I dry her with soft towels, preparing to dress her in simple white linen shrouds. I handle her tenderly aware that I am afraid to touch, afraid that I might catch death, like a cold. As I touch her ankle, I feel a tingle. I stare at her until I imagine her eyes are open and a gentle smile is on her face.

Bubbe Cooks with Fish and Angels

Carrots, fried onions, raw eggs, pike, and carp form a milky mixture. My grandmother's kerchief covered head bends low over the wooden bowl as she chops, shapes dumplings, then, with thick fingers, drops *gefilte* fish into boiling water. Opening her prayer book she faces east, whispers familiar words while the big pot bubbles, steam rising, then disappearing into air. The day before, the carp swam lazy circles in our tub, its mouth a slow series of *o's*.

Bubbe grasps the chicken by its yellow legs, holds on tight, swings it high over my head three times, reciting a blessing with each revolution. I watch its flurry of feathers spread wide, the snow white of wing. I am eight or nine, awestruck that this wild creature, appearing like an angel, is in our apartment.

"To take your sins away," she says.

Later we have it for dinner.

Bubbe prays three times daily, attends services regularly, makes certain our family honors all of Judaism's laws and proscriptions. At barely five feet tall, she oversees kosher, Shabbat, family purity laws, and makes sure we pray too. During the war, she lost first her son, then her husband, and was once beaten bloody by Polish peasants. She keeps her relationship with God intact. I don't know where she keeps her anger.

Epitaph for a Survivor

Bubbe wears a cotton dress, shapeless on her round figure, and a colorless babushka wrapped taut around her head. On her legs thick brown stockings settle into chunky, sensible shoes. On holidays, to dress up, she dons a *shaitle*, a dull brown wig parted in the center then curled into a bun cradled at the nape of her neck. Peering into her crinkled face, etched in branches of age and wear, I see, reserved for me, the curve of a smile, a quiet sparkle of warmth in her brown eyes.

A closer look reveals an unremarkable woman with an extraordinary will.

Fierce in her faith, fiercer still in her determination, living with us she polices the Orthodox directives of our household. Bubbe's Judaism, like a box we all must inhabit, is defined by strict adherence to rules. *We're not allowed*, the words I often hear. I learn when not to mix dairy and meat, which cutlery and dish to use, and not to eat dairy within six hours after consuming meat. When *Shabbos*, the Sabbath, begins on Friday nights, the TV, radio and lights remain off until three stars appear in the Saturday night sky.

Saturdays we walk to services and refrain from work. To avoid initiating "work" Mameh keeps a burner lit on the stove to heat pre-cooked meals. One Saturday I plan to visit my friend, Andy, who lives on the fifth floor of a corner apartment building. *We're not allowed*, Bubbe reminds me, referring to the pushing of an elevator button. Under Bubbe's tutelage, we pray at least twice daily, kissing the prayer book as we conclude. I suspect only Bubbe has her heart in it. When Bubbe *davens*, prays, her Yiddish accented Hebrew words tumble into whispered song. She sways back and forth, then side to side. She's not thinking of Zayde, her husband, or Nussan, her son, one captured in the woods then gassed at Majdanek, the other buried beneath the rubble of a bombed out building. She's no longer in the Bronx. She's in flight. Aloft. Both sparrow and falcon traveling in the hand of her God.

When she is away, Tateh and Mameh argue about her continued presence in our home. Understandable since, adhering to Judaism's family law, Bubbe bans Tateh from Mameh's bed monthly, reinstalling him only after Mameh is cleansed in the *mikvah*, the ritual bath.

I imagine Tateh complies grudgingly, out of respect, duty, or promise. When told they wanted to marry, I can see Bubbe railing against the marriage. I suspect

41

Tateh, never a practicing Jew, agreed to keep an Orthodox household to gain Bubbe's approval. They married
almost immediately after the war. Mameh, likely torn between the two, yielded to Bubbe.

What had passed between them in the woods? I
wonder about the strength of the bond built between the
two women during those two years. Did Bubbe's belief
give strength and assurance to Mameh? Did she convey
protection by the power of personality? Was the rigidity of her will a lifeline? If so, how could Mameh later
separate from her in order to forge her own life? Perhaps
Tateh, darkly handsome, and a proven guerrilla fighter,
offered even greater strength and protection.

Living within the rigidity of religious structure
must have hardened Bubbe's resolve.

She survived.

I am to learn that she carried my cousins, aged
four and six, from dugout to dugout. Steadfast in her belief in God, even while in hiding, she refused to break His
laws, eating only potatoes, *kasha*, bread, milk and cheese
when she could. Never meat. Because they lacked the
resources to properly kosher meat, Bubbe abstained. The
entire time.

She lived with us until Tateh's tolerance ex-
hausted itself. Bubbe moved into Uncle Yitzchaks' Orthodox household, where presumably everyone followed

rules without complaint. There she lived until dementia-induced indignities and nocturnal wanderings forced a move into a nursing home.

She died at age seventy-five.

I see now she was giving me that which, besides her family, she held most precious. That which she would not relinquish, no matter the danger. Her heritage. Only later in life did I come to appreciate that gift.

Leaving the South Bronx

M y parents load everyday dishes, cookware, and
drinking glasses into cardboard boxes. They bun-
dle our clothes into three worn suitcases. The more precious items are carefully wrapped in layers of rags and
stored in the old trunk that traveled with us from Germany. Here are lovingly placed treasures purchased after
the war: fragile porcelain figurines of French courtiers in
ball dress and ballerinas *en pointe*, deep ruby cut crystal
wine goblets, silver flatware and finely etched candelabras, delicate china. Although realizing it strange that my
parents own these treasures, so out-of-place in our shop-
worn immigrant household, I hesitate to question their
provenance. I already know I'll get a vague and unsatisfy-
ing response. Here too are odds and ends, a photo album
my mother carried in a sack during the war, everyday
linens, my German copy of *1001 Arabian Nights*, my old
doll Gerda.

    We're moving north to Pelham Parkway, a work-
ing class section of the Bronx. At eleven years old, I'll

meet girls my age whose fathers are house painters, firemen and taxi drivers, whose families are Polish, Italian and Irish. This time I'll fight with Mameh for the girls' friendship, Jew or not.

Tateh, and Uncle Yitzchak, who owns a grocery store, have amassed enough savings to share this $30,000 home, which I view as the height of American luxury. Surrounded by a modest patch of grass in front and a small back yard, this house, sitting in a quiet neighborhood, boasts identical two-bedroom apartments on two stories, and a ground level studio, offering a rich contrast to our cramped South Bronx apartment. Uncle Yitzchak, Mameh's brother, and his family, are, like Bubbe, strict Orthodox observers of Judaism. Bubbe will live with them on the second floor, while we heathens occupy the first.

Life will be different. No more sirens squealing at all hours, shouts carried from adjacent apartments, thick crowds of people to push through. Maybe Tateh and Mameh will take in the new quiet and let it rest between them.

Maybe Mameh will plant rose bushes like those I've seen in magazines.

Tomorrow is to be a big day. About to burst out of my body, I pace to and fro eager to say good-bye to this apartment's hand-me-down furniture, roach infested walls and dim staircases. Most of all I long to leave behind *Dee Melchomeh*. I'm hoping *Dee Melchomeh* will stay in the South Bronx. With its abundance of random violence, and crush of people, my monster's appetite for chaos might be satisfied here.

I can't sleep. Street noises drift up, car horns blare, sirens wail, people call out to each other. I hear a metallic scraping outside my window, turn to see the familiar outline of fire escape, its iron slats barely visible in the dull blue-yellow light. Then, something else. The dark outline of a man, crouching. Bent low, he clutches something in his hand.

"Mameh!!Mameh!!"

Mameh rushes into the room.

"*Vus ist?*" she asks.

"Over there," I point to the window. Mameh switches on the light.

"*Kik yetz!*"

I look.

The man I saw, a shadow reflected from the shop light across the street, nothing more.

Unable to slow my thoughts, images of the neighborhood recur-of a woman running down the street, shrieking, her shirt torn, breast bleeding; of being chased by four older boys in my stairwell who, snarling obscenities, grab my Hebrew school books and toss them down the stairs; of a little boy struck by a car, his mother kneeling in the street beside him. One image keener than the others: an old woman, her painful gait in stark relief against the rushing crowd is relishing an ice-cream cone. Her hand trembles. It's a crisp sunny day. I sense an aloneness in her that washes over me until I feel I'm drowning in it. Perhaps I will miss this place, so oddly reliable in its familiarity.

Learning to Fly

G od is here, right now. You're not allowed to look,
Feigeh."

I'm under Tateh's *tallis*, his prayer shawl. He,
like the other men on this Rosh Hashanah High Holy
Day has billowed his large white *tallis* over us like one
colossal white wing. During this portion of the service
the rabbi intones the blessing first uttered in the desert
by my father's namesake, the high priest, Aaron, in the
Holy of Holies, the Ark where God was said to have
shown his face. This is the moment when I believe God
is literally going to be here. I sneak a quick peek. I see
the men wrapped in their long *tallit*, heads and bodies
covered. They look like large birds, white against dark
wood of bench, panel, and Ark, about to soar into com-
munion with the Divine. I've heard the face of God is so
overwhelmingly radiant, no one has ever looked and survived. He's not here yet but I 'm not chancing it. I lower
my head and listen.

I'm still young enough to sit downstairs with the

men. This is where the real business, the real voice and movement of prayer are conducted. This is where I sit with my father. I'm surrounded by men swaying back and forth each in a solo dance, fast then faster still, as though they're trying to spin themselves into flight through the Ark and into the vortex of the holy Torah scrolls themselves. My Uncle Yitzchak, my mother's brother is here with his son, Cousin Sruli, and Getzel with his squinty eyes and mischievous grin, and Lame Kallman as he is known, and others, Shmuel the Red, Fat Veftcha, Koppel and Yankel, their names not yet odd to my ear. They are remnants, all of them, survivors, not one American Jew among them. They hum, sing, chant, each to his own rhythm, the raucous sounds swelling the hall are as familiar and comforting to me as the softest lullaby. Like my father, I, too, read from my *siddur*, my prayer book, Hebrew words on one side, Yiddish translation on the other. I don't understand the meaning of the words I'm reading. I think God is not about words. The truth is, God confuses me. Maybe He really won't show up here, just as He didn't in Poland. I know God wasn't in Poland with my parents and their relatives in the forest, otherwise we'd all be in *shul* there on this Holy Day. I know He didn't care that a Torah scroll was kept in my mother's house, so the ten Jews in her village could pray and study in her living room each week. If He did, that Torah and those people would still be there too. So why would

He show up here, on a bright September day in the Bronx? I think maybe God is ashamed to have us see His face. Maybe that's what we're not supposed to see. His absence. What matters to me now, is being here, giving over to the music of chanting and prayer, of ancient words uttered as link to a bent but unbroken chain.

Tateh is *davening*, praying, head bent low over his *siddur*, black skullcap almost disappearing in the coal of his hair, swaying slightly to the music of his prayers. His face is calm today as he licks his index finger to turn a single page. His only past here is a distant one connecting him to desert, to ancestors in flowing robes and sandals, to a God who chooses to be present among His people. Sometimes.

Pretty soon I'll be banished upstairs with the women far away from Torah and Ark. Women may touch or kiss the Torah in deference but are forbidden to read directly from it. Upstairs most women, my mother among them, hold their well-worn prayer books in front of them like afterthoughts only occasionally following along with the men. Most of the women here are as likely to cluck and gossip during services as they are to pray. Children clamber, knees and elbows banging against railing and chair, squealing in play, and add to the cacophony of prayer, song, and gossip. The women's long sleeved dresses form a colorful collage of checks, plaids and flowers, contrasting with the white *tallit* and dark suits of the men. The more pious huddle together near the front of the balcony and ignore the hubbub around them, the *Rebbetzin*, the Rabbis's wife among them. This is where my Tante Basha sits, with her daughter Frances, six years my senior. Wigs bob as the women sway together in prayer like the men. Every once in a while one of the men looks up to the balcony, hisses SSSSSSHAH, which quiets the women and children momentarily.

At twelve I'm a B-movie connoisseur. My current favorites are science fiction movies inhabited by soul mates to our own resident monster *Dee Melchomeh*, The War. The creatures I've seen on screen, nightmares born of atomic fears and apocalyptic disasters, nourish me in their familiarity. I watch whole cities destroyed by giant mutant ants, communities gobbled by nuclear blobs, and am mesmerized by scenes of destruction and chaos. It's real to me. My current favorite is Rodan, The Flying Monster, a fire-breathing prehistoric killer bird, hatched in the post-atomic netherworld of a Japanese cave. Rodan easily dwarfs the towns around him, creates destructive shock waves when flying. In the film he commits suicide after the mortal wounding of his mate, proving what I already intuit. Monster and victim can be one and the same. I know what's possible.

It's three-thirty in the afternoon and I'm in a South Bronx basement room on Washington Avenue, along with six boys my age. Here, in the dim, forgotten space of an apartment building, we attend Hebrew school each afternoon. Hebrew books with worn thumbprinted pages lie open on small-scale oak desks whose surfaces are grooved and scratched with age. The windowless room is stale with odors of penny candy, old books and boredom. Rabbi Jacov, our teacher, looks like the penguins I've seen at the Bronx Zoo. He's wearing his usual black pants and white shirt, sleeves rolled up haphazardly to the elbow. The buttons of his black vest pull and strain against an impressive paunch. Pacing back and forth, he stops at each desk to give assignments for the afternoon, holding a pointer in one hand, stroking his beard with the other. His white beard, streaked with yellow, reminds me of peed-on snow. This year the boys have begun studying for their Bar Mitzvahs, have begun learning to read and chant from the Torah and are grappling with Talmud, Jewish Law. I sit apart, the rabbi giving me passages to memorize from a prayer book, busy work, while he teaches the boys to become learned Jewish men.

"Why can't I study the same as the boys?" I ask for the umpteenth time knowing he'll be plenty annoyed. Maybe the answer will differ this time. He bends down, plastic rimmed glasses sliding to the tip of his nose. He's so close I can see smudges on his glasses, competing there with tiny galaxies of dust motes. Slamming his pointer on my desk, he rasps,

"You're not allowed!"

I've had it. I refuse to disappear into the prayer book yet again. These boys are preparing for the most exciting day of their lives, a day they'll be celebrated and honored, while I lag in shadow. I wait for Rabbi Yacov to go to Eric's desk, see him bend over the old books, point and whisper. I reach into my desk, remove a pencil whose eraser has worn down to metal, take aim and begin to scratch metal onto wood. Covering my working hand with the open palm of the other, I carve, first one line then another. I work quickly. Splinters scatter as I make wood yield to metal - curve, straight line, dot, curve, straight line until form begins to take shape, wing touching wing, body long and sleek, beak in profile. I run my finger over the finished form, enjoying the feel of its rough edges. It covers at least one quarter of the desk.

Rodan, my rescuer. In my fantasy he spreads his scaly wings preparing to whisk me away from this room. Maybe he'll even destroy it. Now, in all his cruel majesty Rodan stares out from my Hebrew School desk, wings tucked, waiting for me to climb onto his back. To fly.

Firefly

A June evening, the sky shifting into a dusty dark blue. The adults gathered in a semi-circle on the green and white plastic chairs Mameh and Tateh had carried out from our garage. My five-year old brother asleep upstairs. Under the sole outdoor light the grown-ups smoke, argue, reminisce. Some bear numbers on their forearms, all bear loss.

I don't pay attention.

I'm twelve and tomorrow will be my birthday. Mameh promised a corsage. Thirteen individual Bazooka bubble gums and one extra for luck, embedded in pink ribbon and tulle, sprinkled with gold sparkles. Tomorrow when I wear it on my wrist the other girls in school will know I'm one of them. A regular American-Bandstand–watching, boy-crazy teen-ager.

Tonight I'm a hunter. My weapon, an empty pickle jar made cozy by a carpet of fresh grass. My prey, the fireflies, just now slow flying within reach. The rhythm and flash of their green lights an easy giveaway in the dark. I reach my jar out, clap my hand over it. There. One, then another. And another. Such easy prey. I've poked holes on the jar's lid so my prey will have a supply of fresh air. Now I sit apart from the adults, on our small patch of lawn, and watch the fireflies I've captured. Their lights flicker on and off.

On and off.

The (un)Anne Frank Diary

January 1, 1960

Dear Diary,

You and I shall become good friends so I'll start off by describing myself. I am 5'31/2" weigh 114 pounds, have short dark hair, wear glasses and braces, am not very pretty, I like boys, and I am Jewish. I am going to be 13 January 12.

Last night (new Year's Eve) I babysat until 4A.M, and made $4. There was mice there and I killed one.

Just off Fordham Road, my best friend Andy and I troll Woolworth's Five and Dime aisles. A mingling of odors blankets us, a heady scent of hot dogs, tuna, chocolate syrup and tomato soup drifts over from the lunch counter. We cruise past the pick and mix candies laid out like semi-precious jewels, past painted turtles sunning themselves near faux palm trees, past crayon colored hair bands, combs and barrettes. Here Andy stops for a moment, reaches for and pockets a comb, in her favorite color, blue.

"Andy," I whisper, "what do think you're doing?"

"Ssshhhh," the reply.

I've studied the Ten Commandments and know Andy just bought herself a lightning bolt.

The truth is I admire Andy her boldness. Sporting movie star looks, a shaggy bob brushes the tops of her smoke filled gray eyes, a petite nose rises gently in the center of her face, and cupid bow lips hint at sophisticated boredom. Unlike the other girls I know, Andy curses, wears white lipstick, and smokes cigarettes. She lives down the street from our house in an apartment building at the tail end of Wallace Avenue. There on the fifth floor, she crams into a two-bedroom apartment with her taxi-driver father, Sonny, bank-teller mother, Shirley, younger sister Suzy, grandmother Nana, and Lady, the dog. Andy is the only person I know to own a dog. Her parents and grandmother are American. Exotics.

Now glancing around until I'm sure no one has seen Andy pocket the comb, I pass sparkling picture frames boasting the frozen smiles of Clark Gable and Marilyn Monroe, of dogs chasing balls caught mid frolic, and of roly-poly babies bubbling delight, until I stop at the stationary supply aisle. Here I see what I want. A diary. I've read and wept over Anne Franks *The Diary of a Young Girl*, and, although I couldn't say it just then, I want to grapple with my secrets and conflicts away from my parents prying eyes in the way Anne did. After all, the

Holocaust breathed down both our necks. Aren't we soul sisters? I will kill a mouse and she died in Bergen Belsen. Death is death. I will come to know it by association and by deed.

I choose a small imitation leather red diary, its edges caressed in gold, its metal clasp insuring privacy, a key its most vital feature, and march it to the cashier.

An Enigma Wrapped in Black

A wild animal.
A wounded bird.
She was both.
She was neither.

As best I can recall it began with a mohair sweater and the testing of my thirteen-year-old push for autonomy. *No you can't tell me what to wear to school today. Not today and not any more.*

I rebelled.
It escalated.
A *Cholera* she cursed in Yiddish.
I held my ground.
She flew into black.

I remember the feel of a broom handle coming down hard on the bone of my right arm.

I remember her face, flushed, eyes wide and the sound of her voice, loud, ferocious.

In Yiddish,

You should die.

In that moment, in my mind, I wished her the same, then made her disappear.

Now, I can reason, and presume.

Maybe she sensed within me, and despised, what lay buried and long gone within her.

Maybe she resented the possibilities ahead for me, my safety, my choices.

Maybe *Dee Melchome* had entered and possessed her.

Maybe she was just broken.

Had I endured what she had what might have become of me?

Passover, Then

"Give this to Tateh," Mameh had said, handing me a bowl filled to the rim. Chunky matzoh balls float in fragrant chicken soup, oily bubbles of *schmaltz* skim the surface of the bowl, steam curls upwards as, walking slowly and mindful of spilling, I present the soup to Tateh. She successively ladles less for my brother, then my best friend, Andy, then me, and lastly serves herself, her bowl less than a third full and holding her favorite delicacy, boiled chicken feet.

Days before Passover, Mameh had readied the old wooden bowl, each year hacking more grooves and fine lines into its mottled surface, creating a kind of hieroglyph record of her labor. For hours, it seemed, she rhythmically chopped pike and carp with the *hackmesser*, then tossed in onions and sweet carrots to form *gefilte* fish. The blade gleamed as Mameh *clop, clopped* on wood, the glint of her wedding band rising and falling with each precise movement of her hand. She reserved the prized fish head for Tateh, its milky eyes to later stare vacantly on his plate.

I've invited Andy tonight who, because her family is secular, will become a Passover *seder* regular. We dress for the occasion in snug skirts and feathery sweaters, believing ourselves sophisticated at thirteen as we stretch rubber bands over our thighs to hold stockings taut, our twin red marks binding us one to the other, like the drops of blood we draw from our index fingers, then ceremoniously exchange, to become "blood sisters."

Our *Haggadot*, free soft-covered booklets distributed by Maxwell House, are no nonsense guides, Hebrew prayers and commentary on one side, English translation on the other. Our booklets have been personalized over time with horseradish and wine stains, with old matzoh crumbs hidden deep within the creases of their spines. Tateh leads the service, rushing through the Hebrew prayers as he competes with the muffled voices of Uncle Yitzchak's family on the floor above. We hear them singing and praying long after we finish our *seder*.

The thick syrupy taste of Manischewitz wine lingers on my tongue after I hook my pinky and gather ten drops. We recite the plagues in unison, *blood, frogs, lice, flies, cattle disease, boils, hail, locusts, darkness, death of the first-born*. The deep vermillion drops shimmer on my plate.

Mameh's voice rises above ours on the word *choshech*, darkness.

Tateh passes a sandwich made of matzoh and

sliced horseradish, its bland crunch and sharp bite mix together in my mouth, the taste of earth and cardboard reminds me not of slaves but the depth of my own hunger.

I notice that on Passover, unlike Rosh Hashanah and Yom Kippur, no memorial candles are lit, that on this holiday none of the adults cry.

I'm eager for Elijah the Prophet's entrance. I believe in Elijah, whose spirit is said to visit each household on Passover, heralding redemption, real peace. Maybe he'll bring peace to our home. A wine-filled goblet rests in the center of our *seder* table to welcome him. When Tateh opens the door inviting him to enter, it signals a moment of awe. I watch Elijah's cup shake as Tateh recites Hebrew words; the wine, I am certain, diminishing in the goblet as Elijah drinks.

As the wine swirls around glass, I notice Tateh's hands underneath the table, shaking it.

After Elijah's welcome Tateh delights in relating a childhood Passover prank. As the door was opened for Elijah in his parents' house, Tateh tells us, he ushered in a goat. Andy and I laugh at the telling, but truthfully, I have a hard time imagining Tateh or his parents, or the goat for that matter.

Towards the conclusion of the *seder*, Tateh now flushed with wine, leads us in song. This my favorite part, our family, sated, relaxed, singing together, ordinary.

Years later with Tateh long gone, Mameh sits on my left as I lead the *seder*. On the table, a cup of spring water, Miriam's cup, is placed alongside Elijah's wine cup. We read about freedom, argue its meaning, and I serve Mameh matzoh ball soup in equal amount to the rest of us.

Roy and Dale Reveal the True American Moral Order

Sucking on a cherry sourball, I sit before the moon-light-silver glow of the box, eyes wide, anticipating the delicious moments to come. Gray and white spots appear, twirling like electronic snow that soon morph into quivering black lines, settling finally into an image accompanied by theme music and titles. Hopalong Cassidy, galloping astride his horse, rides into the foreground, engulfing the screen, seventeen inches and larger than life.

Hopalong wears black, rides his white stallion, Topper, and roams the prairie with his sidekick, Red. Red helps Hopalong annihilate outlaws, shares beans and weak coffee cooked over a campfire, and augments Hopalong's heroic aura.

TV Westerns inevitably include: one cowboy, one sidekick, the hero's white horse, a clutch of bad guys on black horses, fistfights, shootouts and chases, amounting to what is for me, riveting predictability. The good guys always win. The bad guys always lose. It's a world I envy.

I'm captivated by Westerns. Each Sunday evening Roy Rogers, the King of the Cowboys, and Dale Evans, the Queen of the Cowgirls, have lessons to teach. Along with their formulaic plot lines, they offer tantalizing bits of instruction on assimilation. Each episode ends when Roy and Dale ride their horses into the foreground of the screen singing the program's theme, *Happy Trails*.

Happy trails to you until we meet again. Happy Trails to you, keep smiling until then.

These words are essence of American to me. Be happy, keep smiling. The song lyrics hold the promise of permanence; all will be well, as long as one smiles. This then is the American moral order. Trails always lie ahead, inviting order secured by the King of the Cowboys and his six-shooter, the Queen of Cowgirls ever agreeable to the King's wishes. The message could not be clearer or more exotic. This then is what America is about. This is how I imagine real Americans to be, as represented by the King and Queen of the U.S.A., smiling, happy, cleanly shooting outlaws, the bloodless violence quick to excise evil and restore order. The conflicts, the outcomes, are so reliably predictable. A black and white world. How different from home. How different from the Europe my parents knew. The good King and Queen sure to live happily, safe and invincible. Only evil people die. I like this America. If only these capable American cow-folk, who, like Mr. Rosenberg, speak English without a trace of accent, were my parents.

Mamaloshen

Speak English! Why won't you speak English? I shout in my thoughts. English is refined, smooth and polished as marble, Yiddish rough as coal. Shopping on bustling White Plains Road, alongside the rumbling of the El train heading for Manhattan, my parents are speaking, no yelling, in Yiddish. I long to be on that train, going "downtown," instead of here where my parents' voices boom across the avenue. Their Yiddish words form guttural reverberating growls, surely threatening American passers-by, its harshness an embarrassing contrast to the gentility of English.

Right now they are arguing about the price of shoes, about the amount of money spent. Mameh complains he's spent, *tsi fiel*, too much. Tateh flails his arms, *Hahck mir nischt in tcshainik* he thunders, his plaid wool cap bopping precariously on his head. I move a few feet apart hoping they won't notice.

Yelling on the street is their default mode of communicating, the louder the tone, the better. They've no demarcation between inside and outside, between thought and action, between home and the street. They are nothing if not consistent. "Privacy" is a Yiddish word I've yet to hear, "nuance" an alien concept. Closed doors an invitation to barge in, personal mail a free-for-all. A thought pops into your head, spit it out.

Yiddish, the language of cursing, selling, squabbling, gossiping, joking, but rarely, it seems to me, of conversation, rarely of I'll-present-one-idea-and-wait-quietly-for-a-response-from-you-so-we-can-respectfully-exchange-thoughts.

It's a language I'm eager to discard.

And yet.

I hear a softening, a slowing down of voices, a mellowing of tone when I think of my parents sitting around the dining room table with their Lublin immigrant friends, *der Lubliner*, talking about *der heym*, home. The air, dense with the aroma of steaming coffee and sweet cinnamon cake, and thick with cigarette smoke curling up towards the glass-baubled chandelier, carries too a sudden richness in their voices. They're playing cards, gin rummy, the nickels, dimes and quarters strewn around the table. Moments before the house seemed to shake with the racket of their voices, full volume, all talking at once, arguing about the cards, whose turn it is to deal, who won the last hand, arguing, it seems, for argument's sake. Now they're quieter, their Yiddish reverent.

There sits Goldie holding a cigarette between two ruby polished fingernails, and next to her, husband Schmuel, who will soon die of a heart attack, Baila and her husband Yankel of the gentle smile, who will soon be shot and paralyzed inside one of the apartment buildings he owns, and Yosef, *der Shuckler*, the Shaker, whose head twitches and turns in involuntary movement, his war souvenir. And Moishe and Sara, my parents' best friends. From my bedroom, where the walls shudder with the timbre of voices, I hear a hush fall, their Yiddish now cushioned by the thick tones of nostalgia.

"Remember *Grubbe Freyda,*Freyda the Fat?" Goldie asks.

"She made *challah, zees vie tsiker*, sweet like sugar," I hear Tateh say.

They don't speak of Freyda's fate, or their own.

Freyda, suspended in time, whose history ends with the sweet taste of bread.

Der Lubliner conjures people no longer alive, evoke smells and tastes, scenes they recall wistfully that I cannot.

I envy these gentler aspects of *der heym*, that nostalgia infused world I'll never know, those memories of before, before the war, before the decimation of each *Lubliner* family. While *der heym* is not my reality, the open wound of its after courses through me, and not with the sweet taste of *challah*. Dare I say it? I envy their war experiences, the proof of their grit, the solidity of their pain. Like Yiddish, it belongs to them, not me. My fears are empty, inherited without the legitimacy of memory. I feel the terror of their war too, but it rides on the back of a phantom. How can my fears ever measure up to theirs?

Yenta's Ring is Lost then Found

With more than seven years between us, I considered my younger brother a nuisance rather than a fully emerging human being. Besides our parents, we held little in common, and had even less to do with one another. Looking back I recall hitting him, although the circumstances now elude me. I can still see my raised hand, my flash of anger, his tears, but not the provocation, the reason for it. My parents lashed out with leather belts, broom handles and flying hands. I can understand, though not excuse, my own behavior, my anger and raised hand the norm for our family, but my brothers' actions, his apparent desire for punishment, still puzzle me.

"I took it," my brother announces.

I stiffen as the room abruptly hushes, the adults seated around the card table turning to look at him.

"I took Yenta's ring," he repeats, this time louder, with more defiance.

"Vat you do?" Tateh asks, his voice rising as he

lifts himself from his chair.

Yenta, whose diamond ring has been missing since the last gin rummy game, over a week ago, brings her hand to her mouth and lets out a soft *Oy* which makes the massive folds in her body tremble just slightly, a small quake shaking the cosmos before the arrival of after-shocks.

"I said I took it," my brother repeats yet a third time, his face impassive.

"Vat you tell me?"

In an instant Tateh grabs his shoulders and forces him onto the linoleum floor. Crimson faced, eyes bulging and centered on my brother, Tateh removes his belt.

"Vat kind boy is here raised?" he growls, "A *goniff*, a thief, who steals from his parents' friend."

Tateh raises his belt high preparing to deliver the first blow.

My brother cowers on the floor shielding his head with his arm, a posture familiar to each of us. Today is his turn. He knows that to make a sound or move now will bring more anger, more blows. He clenches his eyes.

I can smell the musk of leather, the sharpness of Tateh's rage, my brother's fear.

As the first sharp crack of belt connects with his back, my brother unfolds his arm, winces, then re-veals the faintest trace of a smile, staring Tateh hard in the eyes. As I suspect, he's controlling the beatings. It's happening now, at his bidding, not later, tomorrow or next week. Now.

This brother is a puzzle, unfamiliar to me. The brother I've seen avoids violence at all costs, faints at the sight of a drop of blood, sleepwalks, heading out the door as though anxious to get away. Watching this changeling, I feel tightness in my stomach.

The call comes early next morning while we are finishing breakfast. Tateh reluctantly leaves his plate of herring, sour cream, and black bread to answer it.

"Yah?" he mumbles into the receiver.

He listens and nods, turns to my brother after hanging up.

"That vas Yenta. The ring, she found it in back the couch," he says as he picks up his hat, opens the door and walks out.

My brother is breaking pieces of bread, fingering the black crumbs, swirling them around without purpose.

I pass the herring to him.

Family Euphemisms

Nobody talks about illness in my family. Uncle Yitzchak developed epilepsy soon after the war. I learn about this one afternoon when I return from school to see him lying prone on the asphalt, in front of our lawn, shaking, eyes rolled back. Mameh and Tante Basha flank him, faces furrowed.

"His *peckele*," Mameh says, in answer to my alarmed question. His "little package."

Peckele, also her euphemism for my periods.

Secrets each.

Yitzchak's daughter, cousin Frances, a few years older than I, developed intense pain in her hands. "Arthritis" we were all told. It was not until years later, when she was close to dying, that her son admitted,

"Scleroderma."

As a child, she hid in the woods for two years along with the remnants of our family.

How could she not grow a thick skin?

How could he not quiver?

Flesh

We worship food at my house. Food. Eating it means we're not yet dead. We greet each other not with the conventional, "Hello, how are you?" but with "Have you eaten?" Meaning "Are you vital? Can you run if you have to? Are you still alive and well?" Portliness is the body type of choice, most nights meat, *fleish*, literally translated "flesh," the rarer the better, the staple.

Food battles with my mother continue until I leave home.

"*Ess*," she commands, scrutinizing each bite as I poke the bloodied *fleish*, wrinkled peas and mashed potatoes around my plate.

Leftovers are out of the question. To keep peace, I sneak pieces of *flanken*, *clups*, or steak onto the paper napkin spread on my lap, fold it to fit my palm, and later flush the offending packet down the toilet. As a teen-ager, I strive to be thin, to become speck small. Like *The Incredible Shrinking Man*, I want to transmute into the very cosmos. I eat less, count calories, weigh myself daily.

I didn't know then that I was attempting the skeletal camp survivor look, to experience what my parents had, to be like them, to close the chasm of suffering, disappear.

And have them notice.

Eating *Treyf*

At the end of the meal, Tateh sighs, sits back contentedly, and wipes the last dribbles of lobster sauce off his chin. Our occasional Sunday evening outings to Golden Dragon are one of the few indulgences he allows himself. Before entering, my father looks over his shoulder and pulls his hat low over his eyes. My mother, brother and I slink in behind him. Here in Parkchester, we are far enough away from Pelham Parkway so that we are unlikely to run into any congregants from our synagogue, or worse yet, any customers from Tateh's kosher butcher shop. It's risky business. Being exposed as secret *treyf* eaters would be scandalous, leading at the very least to public humiliation, at worst, financial ruin.

In spite of the risk, Tateh delights in everything about these outings and so do I, traveling together to the restaurant in our old blue Dodge, casing the streets, then stepping over the threshold into a most exotic world. The walls, covered in shocking crimson brocade, so different from our own pale walls at home. An aquarium in the center of the dining room sparkles with fish. Best of all, the rotund and smiling deity at the entrance, greeting the diners. In a Chinese version of the Jewish mantra, this bronze idol seems to be saying *Eat! Eat! It's all right, nothing bad will happen.*

We order following a familiar routine. Every dish includes fried rice, fried egg roll, and ice cream for dessert. I always favor the colorful pistachio ice cream, relishing the crunch of nut chunks embedded in the sweet green concoction.

Tateh and I start with wonton soup, while Mameh, the kosher standard bearer in our family, asks for the egg drop soup, and orders the same for my brother. After much discussion and perusal of the menu, she plays it safe, ordering a chicken dish. Ignoring my school chum Janet's solemn warnings about human body parts sliced into shredded Chinese food, I order Chow Mein. My brother, at six years old, will have an egg roll, rice and a bit of soup.

When it's his turn, Tateh sits straight up in his chair and in thick accent, speaks those four strange words, "Shrimp *mit* lobster sauce." This is not any ordinary *treyf*, with its abundance of shellfish, this is *treyf* to the second power. When his meal arrives he eats lustily, transformed. He melts into the dish, the week's worries dissolving with each bite. Relishing the rubbery morsels, he becomes one with the forbidden lobster sauce, giving himself over to the savory shrimp. He offers Mameh a taste and she, turning up her nose and scrunching down her mouth, says "Worms, *feh*, you're eating worms." Grinning, Tateh takes another bite.

The forbidden food, more than a meal to my father offers a taste of the gentile world, where he can, if only temporarily, give himself over to his senses. In this moment he is no longer an immigrant greenhorn living outside the mainstream. In Golden Dragon restaurant he must feel like a born American. I believe here he suspends memories of his old home, Glusk, Poland, and its degradations and horrors. The few Americans he knows have no such memories. Rather than a denial of Tateh's Judaism the *treyf* seems to represent for him an affirmation of life.

When his health began failing, Tateh learned he needed a heart valve replacement. A surgical success, the replacement extended his life. He remained unfazed when he learned the origin of his donor valve. My father's heart pumped on thanks to the valve of a pig.

Magic Marker

B igger, make it should be bigger," Tateh directs over my shoulder.

I clasp the marker tighter, the black one, to outline, then fill in the fat letters, moving my pen rapidly up and down, crosshatching lines to fill in blank spaces. The red marker lies next to the brown butcher paper. I use it sparingly for emphasis. Finishing, I admire the result,

"Pot roast, sale, 59 cents per lb."

I remember the harsh smells of raw meat and wood chips, of death already settled comfortably into pine. Inside the gleaming glass cases, trays are lined up in rows, forming a palette of reds, whites and grays. My father stands behind glass: cutting, chopping, weighing, wrapping. All along the narrow shop window my handiwork, pieces of butcher paper, some hang like scrolls, each inscribed with the same come hither word:

"Sale."

At home I draw, copying dogs, frowning clowns, a portrait of President Kennedy, and my favorite, Mr. Spock, the Vulcan who has no feelings.

I settle an easel in the basement, away from family, not caring about the quality of light, the north or south of it. Squeezing color from tube, I put brush to canvas, glancing at the open book, *How to Paint*. I copy a painting. A West Indian woman balances laundry on her head, two men beside her, the laundry a pure titanium white, surrounded by hues of rich greens and ochres, rendering clothes, skin. Her features in shadow.

Awash in Blood

Scent of my father, sharp sweet-foul smell of stale blood lingers after he washes and shaves, mingles with other odors: cigarettes, Old Spice, grief. He is soaked in it. Like some ancient Temple petitioner offering the blood of ram to wash sin away. Offering the blood of his daughters, whom, I believed for years, he left in Lublin with their mother, to a certain fate. Does he think he will ever come clean?

Wood chips crunch underfoot. In the freezer, carcasses hang on hooks, fat and muscle whorled splotches of ivory and maroon. Sparkling glass cases hold cuts of loin, lamb, veal displayed like jewels. A bathing beauty sitting beneath a beach umbrella smiles out from the wall, marking days. Tateh wearing his bloodied apron and brown hat, sharpens knives, grinds meat, flirts with his customers.

"Your lips you'll lick," he tells them, saving his complaints for home.

Tateh believes meat ensures health and vitality, is proud to be providing this primal source of sustenance for his family. He likes his meat rare, the blood oozing out onto his plate in crimson rivulets, gristle glistening on bone between flesh.

Dynamic

In the path of Junior High School 135, just a few blocks up the street, students stream by our house mornings and afternoons. The boys solo or in pairs, the girls in clumps, ponytails swinging, clutching books to their chests, chatting, engrossed in each other, oblivious to their surroundings. One afternoon I hear screams coming from the street, in front of our house, in front of the now dormant Rose-of-Sharon tree. Rushing to the window I see my brother, eleven years old, chasing the schoolgirls. Wielding a hammer.

On learning of this Tateh loosens his belt.

Odd for my brother to draw such violence.

He can't tolerate the sight of blood.

No matter how minor.

A band-aid wrapped around a pinky finger

might   spiral him into a dead faint.

No budding butcher he.

But a survivor in his own way.

And his father's son.

My Body Causes Consternation for All

Mameh neglects to instruct me on the particulars of menstruation, as her own mother no doubt also omitted this apparently negligible piece of information. Horrified to see splotches of blood on my panties one afternoon when I am thirteen, I call Mameh who evokes an old East European ritual to ward off evil, and spits three times. She explains I've received my *peckele*, my little package, which will now arrive every month. Like the girdle, this is one package I'm not prepared to receive.

As for Tateh, shaving my legs causes him to erupt into paroxysms of crimson-faced sputtering and exaggerated motions of reeling off his leather belt. Leg shaving is strictly forbidden. The tight fitting sweaters I long for will have to wait as well, until I am at least of legal age.

After much arguing and wrangling between us, I begin dating at sixteen.

I remember Jake, from history class, one of my first dates, arriving promptly at seven to pick me up. We plan an evening at the Paradise Theatre to see Frankie Avalon in *Beach Blanket Bingo*, then on to Jahn's Ice Cream Parlour for dessert. No sooner has Jake crossed our threshold than Tateh begins to chat him up. Benign at first, it soon escalates.

"Vere you live?" he asks, eyebrows raised, head tilted sideways in readiness.

"Vat school you go?"

Within minutes, my father is out of social amenity territory and deep in the woods of Pietchkow circa 1942.

"I vas a *partisana*," he says seemingly out of nowhere, "a guerilla."

I count the estimated seven seconds until his next move.

"I vas shot," he continues, without expression or explanation.

"See."

He turns around to present his back, then lifts his shirt, hooks his thumb into his belt and pulls down to reveal a cream colored six-inch long scar carved into his lower back.

Jake, face flushed, stares at my father's back, shifting weight from one foot to the other. I whisk him out the door.

Gargoyles and Vanilla

At the Paradise, Jake and I enter a grand theatre lobby, gargoyles looming off walls, faces contorted into grimaced smiles. In the center, a well-stocked goldfish pond, its bottom filled with shiny copper pennies, hundreds of wishes submerged with the fish. The strong scent of cigarettes combined with the sharp buttery smell of fresh popcorn hangs in the air, and, as though in minor keys, the unmistakable odors of pomade, Old Spice and Shalimar, which almost masks my own scent, cooking vanilla, two drops dabbled behind each ear. We climb to the upper balcony, to be closer to the ceiling, where a faux star-filled night sky and delicate clouds float above.

The pseudo-romantic surroundings seem to attenuate the distance between us. Sitting next to me in history class, Jake and I had exchanged few pleasantries before he asked for a date. Words between us now seem secondary-we're on a mission, experimenting with dating, with sex. As we watch Frankie Avalon, sleek in a brief bathing suit, sing to Annette Funicello, Jake yawns, stretches his arm out, lets it fall over my shoulder, just brushing my right breast. I stiffen, barely breathing, unsure of what to do, and then feel his hand pull back. I lean into him tentatively, then move away, afraid to breathe, conscious of each rising hair on my neck. We sit stiffly away from each other, our experiment over, as Frankie and Annette frolic amid colorful beach balls and soft sand.

Afterwards, eager to part, we never get to Jahn's.

I return home at an hour that pleases my father, my inexperience intact, an awkward peck on the cheek and quick goodnight from Jake.

Mameh's Gift

Here," she says handing me a blue Alexander's Department Store box, "try on!"

I am confused. Gifts from Mameh always take the form of cash pressed neatly between paper roses and bits of ribbon inside a pink Hallmark greeting card. These cards usually mark birthdays. Mine would not be for another two months. She's just given me a present, a true present, not money, but a thing, an object, like my girlfriends receive from their parents. This is not her style.

"What's this for?"

"For no reason, I went shopping today and thought you could use this," she replies in Yiddish, her face its usual blank mystery.

I take the box, and, with a mixture of hesitation and curiosity, open it, savoring the unfamiliar sound and feel of tissue paper crinkling in my hands. I lift the paper slowly and there, underneath, bearing a price tag marked "sale $7.95" flopping over its edge, lies a folded beige girdle. It resembles a pale, dead fish.

"Go try on," she urges pushing me towards the bedroom.

I slide into the bedroom and wonder how such a tiny piece of material could ever fit over anyone's thighs, hips and waist. I check the label inside. It is indeed my size. Gritting my teeth, I rise to the challenge. I pull and grunt, take a deep breath to flatten my stomach, wiggle my hips and manage to get it on. Clasping stocking to garter, I pull my white slip over hips, then tug navy skirt over that. I cannot breathe properly. Walking is another challenge. The taut material restricts the movement of my legs. When I shuffle into the kitchen, Mameh is smiling.

"Good," she says inspecting me, "you look thin as a movie star."

I rarely wore the girdle my mother gave me. I dusted it off and wore it on my occasional dates, to flatter my figure, I thought at the time. I knew her gift was double edged, an alluring invitation to try on adulthood, to try out what it meant to be a woman, accompanied by the message that somehow I wasn't yet good enough without it, that I needed to be bound.

Liz and Marilyn Reveal Secrets of American Womanhood

The women I know, all European immigrants eager to refashion themselves, possess a kitschy glamour. They follow the marriages of Elizabeth Taylor, the love affairs of Marilyn Monroe, as though acquainted with these icons personally, studying their clothes, make-up, and mannerisms as ideal examples of American womanhood. In their eyes, these movie stars are Jewish by marriage, therefore trusted arbiters of taste and assimilation. My mother, in synch with her woman friends, dyes her brown hair blonde, luxuriates in mink and flashes a diamond ring.

I return home from school one afternoon to find my mother and her friends sitting around the kitchen table amidst a haze of cigarette smoke, half empty coffee cups, and a platter of rapidly disappearing *rugelach* and marble cake.

"Feigeh come here a minute," Mameh says, catching me before I have a chance to retreat.

"We were just talking about Rose's daughter," she continues,

"She dyed her hair last week. You should see how gorgeous she looks!"

"Uh oh," I'm ready to turn on my heel.

"And did you know that Susan M. just had a nose job?" Sara, my mother's best friend, asks referring to a neighbor's daughter.

I retreat into the bathroom, the only room in the house with a decent sized mirror and take stock, wondering whether I'd gain sex appeal by submitting to a surgeon's scalpel and a bottle of peroxide, shamed suddenly by the bump in my nose, my pedestrian brown hair. Still, I resist my mother's suggestions for makeover, preferring to mock her by shunning ruby red lipstick and coloring my lips pale white, substituting flashy clothes for basic black, wearing the mantle of teen-age angst on my sleeve as an anti-Liz, wearing my Jewish looks if not proudly then in firm belief of authenticity. Hollywood, I know, is not the real world. I have no reason to alter my looks.

My evolving teen-age sexual experiences are a blur of brief dates with a succession of boys whose "pants were too short," or "shirts too wrinkled," or who sported some other form of severe maternal violation. We often spent warm evenings on the plastic-covered lime green living room couch, my parents ostensibly asleep in their bedroom down the hall, the proverbial girdle offering its own unique barrier, a mid-twentieth century chastity belt requiring some deft maneuvering; the couch's plastic, another barrier, sticking to our legs. I remember the local "make-out" spot; a deserted stretch along City Island packed during dark summer nights with Chevys and Dodges lined up in rows. I recall the lap of waves in the distance, the furtive groping and wet kisses, the thrill of the forbidden, the sudden glare of police flashlight shining harshly in our eyes. As far as I knew, real adult sex, "going all the way," was limited to the girls who shunned academic classes in high school, the girls whose hair was a bit too teased, whose skirts a bit too tight, whose make-up a bit too loud, and yes, who even wore girdles daily.

Don't Tell

Climbing the stairs to the elevated train that will rumble and roll me away from the burnt out buildings and blackened windows of the South Bronx, away from Pelham Parkway, past Simpson Street through Manhattan's tunnels to Twenty-Eighth Street, I believe that once alighting in the heart of the garment district, I'll emerge transformed, the subway-train a steel capsule speeding me towards a new life, one of my own making, clean, glitzy, safe.

Commuting from home, I board the number two express train that rattles downtown. I travel during "rush hour," a euphemism for the crush of bodies piled together in intimate proximity on their way to and from work. The stale air smells of sticky-sweet perfume, yesterday's sweat, old newsprint. A man presses against my back, pushing himself further into me as the train dips around a corner. I tense my body. Subway accident or purposeful lunge? Would it be rude to say something? What would I say? It's a while before I catch on. Only men squeeze against me. Never women. One day a spiky stiffness wedges against my lower back. When I turn to peer at the man standing behind me, I'm met with a blank stare. On the subway the following day I maneuver an oversized black plastic portfolio behind my back, already armed with stickpins.

At age sixteen I dream of becoming a fashion illustrator. I hope to draw those slim, improbably long-limbed women posing in furs, A-lined dresses, pill box hats, and silky lingerie, who glamorize the margins of the New York Times and divert attention from Cuban missiles and Birmingham Alabama water hoses. Lackluster grades prohibit my acceptance into one of the city colleges, my parents' choice for me. (Become a teacher then marry, the Bronx mantra of the day). My folio of clowns, animals and portraits of pop icons *au currant* is deemed worthy of entry into lower Manhattan's Fashion Institute of Technology, my temple of art and glamour.

Approaching the building that first September day, I see it sits squat, a rough slab of raw concrete and glass. Its sleek architecture, in a style I later discover labeled Brutalism, so unlike the drab Bronx homes I'm accustomed to. The cool artistic sensibility of the place I imagine key to the shedding of my roots, to my wearing the moniker "artist," and beginning life as an illustrator with a chic Manhattan career, the weave of my immigrant past shredded and gone.

Inside the lobby, plaited textiles, the colors of earth and sun, are encased behind glass, as in a museum. Mannequins pose gazing intently at nothing, hands on hips, in shimmering gowns of organzas and satins, whose colors range from crimson reds to deep midnight blues. They pose too in day clothes, a whirl of shirtwaist and seersucker dresses, bouffant silks, shirred, swing and pleated skirts, all cut precisely at the knee.

My own clothes are typical Alexander's Department Store issue. Walking down the hall to life drawing class in my cable stitched cardigan and plaid skirt, I'm out of step with girls parading in oversized chunky sweaters over pencil skirts, and slacks with stirrups.

Later that first day, assembled in the auditorium for orientation, we're asked to look left, then right.

One of the three of you won't be here next semester, we're told.

In life drawing class, we stand at easels, charcoal in hand, encircling the models. Naked women, some with bulbous breasts and round bodies, others pencil thin, one with a tampon string hanging below her pubic hair, pose, contorting their bodies for one minute quick sketches, sitting in repose on velvety draped fabric for an hour's study. The men, more modest, wear thin jock straps. Anxious about the casual display of flesh, about competing with my classmates, I hunker down behind my easel. I try to draw with the bold surety of line I recognize in the New York Times illustrations; aiming to acquire the bohemian sophistication I envy in the other older students, to be like them - individualists. The young men and women whose lids are drawn over eyes that barely mask boredom, haughtiness, self-assurance.

Squeezing charcoal between thumb and forefinger in fashion illustration class, I will lines onto cheap newsprint paper to render a curve of hip, a drape of skirt, a delicacy of hand. My lines ooze thick, labored, tight onto the muddied paper. My rigidity an effort to hold the slippery, frightened parts of myself together. I'm overwhelmed by fears. My body sometimes shakes with them. Fears I can't always name. Often, I recall of that fall semester, are days I yearn to hold my breath until I evaporate.

One November day class is interrupted. A young man enters with an announcement just heard on the radio.

"The President's been shot. We don't yet know his condition."

We wait anxiously for more information, and, when the inevitable news is delivered, are sent home. There is no rush hour on the train that day. No need for a portfolio behind my back. The dazed silence is splintered by the quiet sobs of a teen-ager, a young black girl, shrunk into an oversized jacket, her tear streaked face a repository for us all. If the young President is vulnerable to assassination, what about the rest of us? Who will protect us now from dark forces swirling constantly, seeking anchor. Those forces that might generate a rifle shot, a snarling dog, a slashing knife, an atomic explosion, a swastika, a raging parent. Who will protect me?

I fail fashion illustration.

I'm called into the dean's office and asked to leave.

One of the three of you won't be here next semester.

Leaving my portfolio behind I walk down the hall and out the building. I hear the screech of brake and churn of rail somewhere in the distance and fly into a dark tunnel. I try to summon Rodan. Rodan would whisk me away. But I am alone. Rodan can't reach me here. I feel my feet touch ground. But is it ground, or air, or sky? I can't tell. A bite of Bronx early winter chill. I'm home. Home and lost. Mameh is out shopping, Tateh at his butcher store.

Failure dooms me to the life set out for me. Marriage to an accountant or tradesman, an apartment on Bronx River Parkway, two sullen children, plastic covered furniture, spiritual death. I have no skills. No future. I'm tired of being afraid. Tired of failing. My longing to separate from my parents dashed, I want to blanket myself in oblivion.

I remember the pills. Aspirin are the only pills

in our medicine cabinet. Reaching for them I grab a handful, wash them down with cloudy tap water, climb into bed and wait for black. I close my eyes and it's night inside my head.

Later when Mameh comes home I'm conscious still.

"What are you doing in bed?" Mameh asks.

I tell her.

"*Bist du mishuguh?*"

"Are you crazy?" she gasps between sharp intakes of breath.

A flustered phone call summoning Dr. Kossak, our family physician, just down the street.

After he leaves with assurances to my health,

"Don't tell Tateh," she says.

And, faithful to our family dynamic of silence, no more was said.

Afterwards, I bounce from a brief unsuccessful stint in secretarial school, to a series of part-time jobs, a memorable one billing women for illegal abortions, another stealing designs for a bra factory. After several semesters of night courses I matriculate full time to Hunter College, a short bus ride away. There I major in psychology, secretly hoping to learn whether my fearfulness is a sign of insanity, my failures a syndrome.

Aquarius Rising

I can smell freedom waiting out there, beyond the endless rows of boxy Bronx houses, beyond the patches of tired lawn and provincial thinking. Freedom–its seductive aura carried uptown from Manhattan on East River tugs, the rumbling cars of the El. Freedom is the scent of a breeze wafting through sultry city nights, carrying traces of each neighborhood it has passed: here the pungency of garlic, there, the sweetness of Central Park magnolia blossoms, elsewhere the sharp acid of overflowing trash and bus fumes.

It's the aroma of tangy oil paint and earthy clay waiting for the hand to form it.

It's freedom to lose my virginity.

Life looms.

I find a studio apartment on the outskirts of Greenwich Village. Its skylight and sleeping loft appeals to my nascent aesthetic. Looking at my patch of sky from high up in bed, I imagine I can reach up to touch it, and touch possibilities boundless as the sky.

The two hundred and fifty dollar per month rent is equal it seems to the number of roaches nightly invading my kitchen. These roaches don't disgust me in the way the roaches in our South Bronx apartment did. Perhaps I feel ownership. My apartment, my roaches. Mine. I call an exterminator, spread baking soda on the floor. It's a losing battle. The critters and I make peace.

My street hosts a Salvation Army building, a Greek *souvlaki* stand, a church. On Saturday nights, young men spill out onto the street. I hear their drunken shouts and watch punches fly from my fifth floor window, their blows often continuing until, sirens screaming, police arrive.

Sunny days I walk to Washington Square, strolling past small time drug dealers, to watch old men play chess on concrete checkerboard tables, and hear beatniks espouse poetry and play bongos. It's the artists I admire, mostly shaggy young men sketching on pads of paper, and painters working *plein aire*.

I meet George in a photography class, on an outing to the Brooklyn Bridge. On a summer's evening we shoot its vast steel girders arching gracefully above us, expansive, beautiful, inviting.

We become lovers.

I acquire a Siamese cat, name him Ramah.

I listen to Joni Mitchell, Dylan, Cat Stevens.

When she arrives on the scene Janis Joplin becomes my favorite. I admire her blistering voice, her woundedness transformed into art, her fuck you attitude.

I read RD Laing, Carlos Castenada, Gunter Grass, and Abbie Hoffmann, who exhorts me to steal his book.

I try LSD, pot, cocaine. I like LSD best.

I march on Washington, protesting Richard Nixon's inauguration.

I join a women's consciousness-raising group, where we complain about men, and talk about learning to love our bodies; a task presumably helped along by examining our vaginas with hand held mirrors, and tasting our menstrual blood.

I no longer wear a bra or shave my legs and underarms.

I discover Helen Epstein's *Children of the Holocaust* and learn that we, the second generation, share a syndrome, its symptoms familiar as my mirrored face. We view the world as dangerous (anxiety our default mode of being), and our parents as needing protection. While not sharing our parents' experiences, we have acquired their trauma. Many were raised in silence with secrets more secret than sex.

I am not alone.

I write Epstein a letter of gratitude.

She doesn't answer.

Validation is no guarantee of release.

The Appeal of Skid Row

To say my parents are unhappy with my independence would do them an injustice. When I tell them I plan to move to Manhattan, they threaten, curse and wail that I'd bring shame on the family. But they adjust, periodically coming to dinner, bearing gifts of meat and money, despite my protestations. As I settle into a life so different from theirs, the divide between us deepens. In Manhattan, I feel firmly rooted in my time and my place. Looking back I see how rooted I was in theirs as well.

As a young Jewish woman of the 1970's I'm expected to choose between teaching and social work as an occupation. The real work, the true expectation, finding a husband, settling into a sterile suburban home, and raising children. This I have no desire to do. I follow the proscribed path, in part at least, after college, working first in child services, later as a welfare worker for the N.Y.C. Social Services Department. I quickly tire of gray–steeled windowless bureaucracy, of the mass of endless paper work. I want to work with people vilified by society, not fill out forms. I scan want ads.

"Innovative new program seeks caring, experienced caseworker to counsel alcoholics."

I get the job.

Housed in the Men's Shelter on East Third Street, a six story brick building teeming with men in various stages of debilitation, drunkenness and decay, the Manhattan Bowery Project is a humane medical model for treating alcoholism as a disease. Its forty-eight-bed ward offers a voluntary alternative to jail or flophouse, the first of its kind detoxification unit. I will be counseling the men while they're drying out. Here is an opportunity to help society's outcasts, to humanize the lowest of the low. It isn't Nazi Germany, but close enough. I can intervene. Maybe save a life.

"Why do you drink?" I ask Lang, an Oglala Sioux, the requisite question after his third admission to the ward. He stares blankly at me. His long black hair streaked with one shock of white speaks of trauma, hurt, history.

"Tell me about yourself," I forge on ignoring sparks shooting from his dark eyes.

He never does. Secretly I admire his silence, his proud stubbornness, the suffering of his people, all so achingly familiar.

I don't want to be like my European parents and their wounded circle, who wear their narrow views, their explosive tempers, their unfathomable pain like coarse overcoats, the burn of fabric scratching, constantly scratching against tender skin, that skin raw and untouchable. My skin is tender too. I want to protect it. Expand it.

One icy night a co-worker and I huddle in graffiti covered doorway, and, shivering, share a bottle of brandy.

"If they could see us now," I say. We giggle.

We are single, lonely. They, these outcasts, now the hub of our lives. Whom are we trying to save?

Days I counsel Bowery men, nights I dip brush into Winsor color, hand in wet clay, or photo chemicals (transforming blank paper to image, the bath a sweet-sour vinegary smell), attend a sculpture class on St. Marks Place, fantasize about marrying an artist. I will inspire him, warm him in our cold garret, cook soup, mix paints from pigment.

In the thick of it, I don't see a connection between welfare mothers, the homeless Bowery alcoholics I'm tending and the vilification of my own parents. Although I'd like to, I can't erase my parents past, salve their wounds, at least not directly. Perhaps I can by proxy.

When I talk to the patients, I often recognize in them some dark shadow corner of my own. I know about the corrosive effects of failure, its gradual wearing down of confidence, self worth. Aren't I too a disappointment to my family? Haven't I failed by age twenty-two to achieve expected landmarks, marriage, children, staying close to home?

If the men can't love themselves, I'll show them they are worth loving. I'll be their cheerleader. If they can't stay sober on their own, I'll point the way: AA, Antabuse, work programs, inpatient rehab, or counseling with me if they stay sober on their own.

The danger attracts me too. These men live on the edge, as likely to be stabbed in their sleep, run over in the street while in a stupor, as they are to succumb to the ravages of alcohol poison. Teasing death. I see now reverberations of the Polish woods and the dangers to life there. Unlike Poland, here is a struggle I can referee, maybe alter.

Looking deeper into shadow I feel superior to these men, smarter, healthier, and enjoy wielding power by whipping them into shape with my words. *Superior? Whipping them into shape?* These words jump out at me as I write them. There's an echo of the familiar here. The psychological term, identifying with the aggressor. Perhaps some part of me plays Nazi to their Jew, perpetrator to their victim, so as not to feel powerless myself. A preferred stance, being powerful. Or a comfortable illusion.

Missing

In painting class, I render still lifes; apples and pears set in front of pale blue ceramic pitchers, or dreamy nudes splayed on lush drapery. In a rented studio where a furnace belches in one corner I tack raw canvas and paper on a twelve-foot wall. On them screaming men emerge, arms outstretched Christ-like against murky waters. I paint single figures missing limbs, odd animals, and, from photographs, Mameh.

My mother's portrait captures her cloud of gray hair, fine as mist, a bold curve of nose, hard set of mouth. Facing straight out, her eyes blank, in place of iris and pupil, I fill empty space with a gray-blue wash, that space an enigma, far away from me, one I yearn to know.

As a young woman, I longed to have Mameh tell me I'm pretty, to help me unravel the mysteries of my body, of sex. But,

Mameh is missing many things.

Her gold bracelet, a gift from my brother.

A finger severed at the joint in childhood.

Her Mentow home.

Her father, brother and uncle.

Her cousins.

Pleasure.

Years later, rummaging through old paintings, I find two self-portraits. In the smaller, I stare out full frontal, eyes wide as in surprise, my head reaching beyond the canvas boundary, squeezed into the space. The second portrait, rendered in expressionistic style with harsh strokes and bold line, holds my notice. Here, in a palette of blues, ochres, crimsons, black and white, is a three quarter view emphasizing my curve of nose, hard set of mouth and eyes in a gray-blue wash lacking form or depth. My hair, curly and shoulder length, already streaked with lines of white.

Missing is any hint of softness, of pleasure.

Scooped Out and Numb

After three years on the Bowery followed by two sluggish years of social work school I land a job in a psychiatric clinic. At the end of three more years I no longer care to plumb the depths of depressed women, psychotic teenagers, explosive drug addicts, lost souls. I'm scorched, scooped out and numb. I quit and settle on a union job with AT&T, strap on a tool belt, exchange line tests with installers. Easy work, it's mechanical, undemanding. The verbal interchange required with installers and mapped out in our manuals limits conversation to wires, tones and electrical shorts.

After work each evening I run.

I run to dull my thoughts.

I run to shut out the world.

I run circles around Central Park, strengthening my body, imagining a swift escape from the city if I needed to get away in a hurry. From fire, invasion, nuclear catastrophe or neo-Nazis.

I can outrun them all.

THE BUTCHER'S DAUGHTER

At night I sleep with a knife under my pillow.

I take lovers, sensitive men in the arts, introspective therapists, a judge, a shopkeeper, a doctor, a drifter, all short term.

After some weeks or months, I hear the thunder of a steel door crashing shut somewhere inside myself.

The outcome always the same.

"It's not working," I say.

"I'm busy," I say.

"Good-bye," I say.

Blackout

One evening Lower Manhattan is blacked-out, the subways stalled. After work, I lace up running shoes, don running shorts and tank top, stuff work clothes into my backpack and begin a slow jog uptown. The East River, shimmering in twilight, is dotted with tugs and barges appearing to groan under their loads. I pick up my pace as a man approaches alongside and attempts to spark a conversation. Ignoring him, I run faster. Keeping pace, he persists. He, too, is running home on account of the blackout. He tells me about his work, travels, military background. Peering out of the corner of my eye, I notice he's older than other men I've known, that he's running in a rhythm of resolve, planting one foot firmly in front of the other, plop, plopping as though he fully owns his space. Several miles later, we exchange phone numbers, agree to meet again for a running date.

His name is Joe.

Island

I am being "courted," a word Joe likes to use as though we're characters in a Victorian romance novel. With eleven years between us, we bear generational differences. I like wearing long Indian skirts and peasant blouses, stash marijuana in a jar labeled "oregano," and liberally sprinkle my language with curse words. He wears tailored suits, sports gentleman's habits, walks curbside to protect me from errant splashes of mud, opens doors, and pulls out chairs for me with a flourish and sly smile. I find Joe's gentility both endearing and alien. My nascent feminism urges me to scoff and resist, but secretly I inhale his attention and romantic nature.

A maitre d' who drips obsequious banalities greets us at the Box Tree restaurant, a Manhattan brownstone hideaway adorned with heavy burgundy curtains, dark wood, and soft lights. In this intimate space I look around and learn to name new objects--Tiffany glass panels, Viennese Art Nouveau vases, Wedgwood china, Christofle silverware. A crimson rose rests on each of our china plates.

We order sorrel soup, *croustade* of scallops in champagne sauce and conclude our meal with delicate greens, sweet pears and blue cheese accompanied by vintage port. Bowing slightly the maitre d' delivers a black phone tableside for Joe's business calls. Drunk on lust we hold hands beneath candlelight and melt into each other, a prelude to the nights other pleasures.

In the restroom I find gold fixtures, pink rose petals floating in a silver dish, a sharp citrus perfume in a crystal bottle, and crisp hand linens monogrammed in lush thread. I'm in a foreign country, a fairyland. Any moment my lady-in-waiting will appear to comb my curly brown hair and fuss over my dress. I wash the grittiness of Grimm's down the sink and emerge, not as the daughter of war-ravaged immigrants, but as Cinderella to my All-American Prince Charming.

I like this story. I like its sensuality, its floating-on-air magic. Its serenity. This land tastes of Turkish Delight, sweet, sharp, exotic, dissolving the taste of ash and fear.

I learn to accept Joe's gifts-dinner, jewelry, safety. He values me.

A former spy, he knows how to kill with the well-placed twist of a ballpoint pen. I pull the knife tucked for years under my pillow and return it to the kitchen where I simmer stews in the cold of winter.

As natural as the turning of seasons Joe, firmly in

my life, transforms my "I" into "We."

We run the six-mile loop around Central Park every evening in lockstep and slowly reveal our lives to each other. We shower, have dinner, spend nights together.

I learn that Joe, a rascal and slacker as a child, gained acceptance into the Naval Academy, became a peace activist, then a buttoned-down executive. He hunts wild boar in Turkey and loves to bake. I learn about his three adult daughters. I learn he loves children.

He accepts with amusement my status of former-psychiatric-social-worker-turned-tool-belt-toting-AT&T-employee. I laugh and groan at the relish with which he spins bad puns. I teach Joe (not always successfully) to respect his inner life, to accept and acknowledge his feelings, a revelation to a disciplined ex-military guy not expected to have or show feelings.

We travel.

In January we sail the British Virgin Islands, island hopping until we arrive in paradise, Moskito Island. A private island off the coast of Virgin Gorda dotted with secluded beaches it boasts the best chef in the Caribbean and accommodates two-dozen guests. A few people cluster at the bar. Another handful lie scattered like seashells on an ivory colored beach. We're soothed by the soft sounds of palm leaves that sway like slow dancers in the tropical breezes. I curl my bare toes around warm white sand; give myself over to Joe and the cerulean sea.

One day we hike a trail snaking from our cottage along sandy coves, and rest in a small meadow, alongside a beach sheltered by cliffs. We lie side by side on soft grass, the sun warming us. We could be the only two people in the world. I'm at peace.

Under a wide blue sky Joe turns toward me, wraps me in his arms and asks, "Will you marry me?"

Yes, oh yes.

Picnic at Bish Bash Falls

Joe and I mark our engagement by inviting my parents to a picnic at Bish Bash Falls, a verdant area outside the city known for its spectacular waterfalls. Eager to ease their acceptance of Joe, I plan a low-keyed afternoon. Tateh has already scowled his displeasure during the ride and ignored Joe's attempt at conversation. Mameh dons an immutable face. For them Joe's prior marriage and grown children are anathema, his Protestant upbringing a disgrace.

We arrive on a spring day when the air brushes our skin with fresh warmth. Families and couples relax on blankets laden with bold colored coolers, whose crimsons and deep blues, like flags planted on newly triumphed land, herald the arrival of this vibrant season. Children's squeals combine with the buzzing of bees, the throaty call of birds, the rustle of young leaves. The sun streams through dappled leaves forming a mosaic of light and shadow. We choose a spot not far from the parking lot to lay down the old blue blanket designated as our picnic tablecloth, and unpack the cold chicken, salad, fruit and wine. Joe and I make small talk as we eat and attempt to include my parents.

"*Ich gehe spatzieren,*" Tateh says ignoring our efforts to spark conversation.

"I'll go on the walk with you," I offer.

We cut through the parking lot towards the waterfalls when Tateh stops. A red Volkswagen steers wide circles around us, its movements random, erratic. It circles once, twice and yet again. A young man at the wheel looks no older than sixteen, a middle-aged man beside him. Tateh stands transfixed, rooted to cement, his eyes wide, his jaw slack.

When the car circles within feet of us a fourth time, Tateh, his face ashen, cries out,

"*Sie vehl mir derhagenan,*" and, with me trailing behind, lopes towards the safety of our blanket.

"Tateh, you're wrong. No one wants to kill you. They were probably practicing so the kid could get his driver's license."

I offer him wine, which he drinks in great gulps.

"I practiced driving with my daughters in parking lots too," Joe offers.

Tateh turns to look at him.

I realize then how dangerous still the world is for Tateh and mark my own fears-marrying Joe, oddly, not among them.

Something Old, Something Blue

Mameh in blue silk and pearls stands on my right, Tateh, his mouth half open, eyes dazed, on my left. Joe, smiling, waits under the flowered canopy. Just before we walk down the aisle, my mother with tears welling and a hint of bitterness, whispers,

"You're going to have such a better life than mine."

I feel the long stems of French tulips twist and strain in my arms.

II

Dee Melchome

Prose Villanelle for a Guerilla

In the last photo of us together, at my wedding, smiling relatives dance in close circle around us. Tateh's hand reaches under my hair, his mouth on mine, not like a father; I recall it more desperate, reminding me of a spurned lover. My left hand, freshly forged band on ring finger, extends to his shoulder, to touch him.

I phoned them from our Vermont honeymoon inn. At the time, this did not seem at all strange. Tateh and Mameh had longed for my marriage, for the promise of grandchildren, the ascent of new life from ash. I anticipated words of joy, of congratulations.

"A wedding that wasn't. It was a business meeting," Tateh seethed slamming down the phone.

The call came as Joe and I, celebrating our two-week wedding anniversary, were finishing dinner. On the table, thank you notes to be addressed and mailed.

I heard the doctor's words in fragments:

"Your father... blood clot... lungs...I'm sorry."

Pouring a glass of wine, I took stock.

Nothing. I felt nothing.

"Heat, she won't give me heat, so cold it is here. To kill me she wants. To shove me into my grave. I'll bury her first. I'm leaving her. Let her freeze by her own self," he said, words tumbling rapidly, the timbre of his voice registering real fear. The last time I heard that voice.

"Here, you talk mit her."

"*Meshuguh* he's become. Crazy, like I don't know what. Let him leave, that *meshugunner*. Maybe then I'll have some peace," she hissed. I pictured her nostrils flared, her fists clenched, her knuckles milky against the coal black of receiver.

They argued about Mameh's refusal to turn up the heat, the lack of warmth a barometer for the ice crusting year after year between them. Twirling the cord around my index finger, I listened for some minutes, and after acknowledging each grievance, convinced Mameh to power up the furnace. Miles away and newly married that was all I could do.

In the last photo of us together, at my wedding, smiling relatives danced in close circle around us. Pallid and thin, just months after surgery, Tateh had shrunk into himself, whittled down to an essence he seemed hollow as a shell. His hand, the hand that for years had torn cow's flesh from bone, that wielded leather and fist, reached under my hair, his mouth on mine, not like a father; I recall it more desperate, reminding me of a spurned lover. My left hand, freshly forged band on ring finger extended to touch his shoulder, now air and brittle cartilage in place of muscle and heft. On his mouth, the familiar taste of loss, bitter, again.

"In Poland I vas a gorilla," Tateh often told me when I was a child.

Once I'd seen my father naked. He was hairy, but not furry. I had many questions then. When did he change into human? Did a witch cast a spell? Had I been a gorilla too? Gorillas in the zoo didn't resemble my father at all. They were big like my father, but I didn't think they cried in their sleep as he did. I don't recall when I realized Tateh was a warrior, a guerilla, nor do I remember attaching meaning to the word "guerilla" beyond images of Che Guevera, or the Viet Cong perhaps, but not Tateh, certainly not Tateh.

I was twenty, at Yad Vashem, in the Hall of Remembrance, the Holocaust memorial in Israel, overcome by the stark magnitude of its effort to memorialize millions. Wandering through its archives, I found an English book about Jewish partisans, a simple hardbound book, not unlike a high school textbook, its title lost to me now, and in the index, Tateh's name, Aaron Grende, directing me to a short paragraph describing his leadership of a band of partisans in the forests of Poland.

Because of that book, the words "guerilla" and "Tateh" coalesced. Because of that book, I felt pride. Tateh was proud too when I later told him. "Feigeh, she found my name in a book in Israel," he'd brag. That was all. The words "guerilla" and "Tateh" still remained hollow concepts. Until I found his story years later, in a dim, dust-filled Warsaw archive room.

We sat at our dining table after the call, Joe and I, absorbing the moment. The thank you notes forgotten. Dr. Kossak lived a few houses away from my parents. When I was younger, he'd arrive black leather bag in hand within minutes of a call, to tend to a high fever, cramps, fainting spells. It had been years since I'd seen him. His tone had been matter-of-fact:

"Your father...blood clot...lungs...I'm sorry."

Pouring a glass of wine, I took stock.

Nothing, I felt nothing.

Tateh liked to show the scar along his lower back to the boys I dated. *I vas partisana. Shot,* he'd say, with barely a how-do-you do, almost as soon as the hapless boy crossed our threshold. Tateh then raised his shirt, and presented his back, the ivory scar deep, jagged and long. I've often wondered what Tateh meant to convey. He clearly established dominance; my dates left speechless or sputtering. Why direct the young man to his wound? I knew he was binding me to that scar too, his motives a mystery. I knew, too about his other scars, the gaping wounds still fresh and oozing, the invisible scars just beneath his skin. The ones he never talked about.

Tateh's eyes registered as pools of dark liquid longing each time he looked at me. I had to shield myself. Make myself numb. His gaze, the intensity of it, and the quantity of tears I imagined he held in check seemed to span oceans. I became sand to that ocean, dry, porous, flat.

In the last photo of us together, at my wedding, smiling relatives dance in close circle around us. Tateh's eyes, the emptiness in them, shielded in profile. Tateh's hand reaches under my hair, his mouth on mine, not like a father; I recall it more desperate, reminding me of a spurned lover. My hand freshly forged band on ring finger, reaches for his shoulder, to touch him. On his mouth, the familiar taste of loss, bitter, again.

Tateh didn't speak about his children, my sisters. When he looked at me, I saw reflected back in those dark pools of longing three of us-a triad of two phantoms, and a living child. All three of us objects of his desire, reminders of his loss, to lose and lose again; in his nightmares, his thoughts, in his reality. I believed he had left them in the ghetto. To fend for themselves while he ran into the woods, becoming a guerilla leader, blowing up Nazi trains, protecting forest families. Surviving.

Afterwards, when he was sure they were dead, he kept his silence, making a home for them in both the well of his eyes and in my breath. Binding us all together.

The phone rang in the middle of the night. One o'clock. Three a.m. I wasn't sure. Tateh was screaming. Incomprehensible. "It's the middle of the night," I mumbled holding the phone away from my ear. His wails pierced the wires.

"The Angel of Death was here," sobbing now.

"What do you want me to do? I'm far away."

I drifted off. In the morning, not sure whether I'd been dreaming, I called Tateh, relieved to hear his voice, cranky, as usual. I had not yet heard those other words.

"Your father... blood clot... lungs...I'm sorry."

I can still see the table Mameh's set in honor of Joe's first dinner at their house. We've just become engaged. She's laid out the fancy gold-rimmed china and heavy silver flatware, the cut crystal glasses, all from Germany. Only the coarse white paper napkins, creased into triangles on the embroidered linen tablecloth, a reminder of Mameh's village roots. Joe, an old fashioned kind of guy, emerges from the back room, where he's just asked Tateh for my hand in marriage (a quaint custom, I thought at the time). Tateh makes no mention of their conversation.

In the center of the table, a platter of turkey,

already carved, the pieces splayed helter-skelter, surrounded by thick slices of jellied cranberry sauce, *kugel* and boiled broccoli. Mameh passes the platter to Joe, who chooses a plump drumstick, its skin perfectly crisp. Tateh watches closely as Joe lays it on his plate. In an instant, Tateh, reaches over, snatches the drumstick with his fingers and, with a flourish tosses it on his own plate, announcing,

"That's mine."

In the last photo of us together, at my wedding, smiling relatives dance in close circle around us. Tateh's hand reaches under my hair, his mouth on mine, not like a father; I recall it more desperate, reminding me of a spurned lover. My left hand, freshly forged band on ring finger, extends to his shoulder. My outstretched fingers suspended, my link to him permanently frozen in midair.

An ordinary day. Just like any other. Up in the morning Tateh would have showered. Shaved. Breakfasted on black bread slathered with butter and prune jam. Sipped instant coffee, dark, with three teaspoons of sugar. Perhaps read the Yiddish *Forward*, or visited his good friend Schmuel, two blocks away. They might have gossiped. Consumed more coffee. Late afternoon, waiting for dinner, he would have hoisted his feet up, relaxing in his brown upholstered recliner. On TV, wrestling, maybe a Yankee baseball game. Then nothing. A black hole. No time to think. No fear. Almost certainly no pain. A blessing.

For months afterwards, I heard Dr. Kossak's words in fragments:

"Your father... blood clot... lungs...I'm sorry."

The words jumbled together then broke apart, their meaning echoing from some distant place.

Nothing. I could feel nothing.

They Didn't Kill Us All

My brother and I sit in front of Rabbi Sternberg, in a windowless room, door closed to the small crowd quietly congregating outside. There, Joe waits with Mameh, trying, I imagine, to comfort her.

"What do you remember?" he asks. "What kind man he was?"

My brother and I glance at each other, then stare blankly at Rabbi Sternberg who is about to deliver the eulogy.

We are at a loss for words.

I feel his disapproval, his silent accusations.

Later at the service Mameh, sitting between Joe and me, seems small and eggshell fragile. In lieu of ripping our clothes, a symbol of mourner's anguish, an ancient custom, Rabbi Sternberg has pinned torn black ribbons onto our collars, right side representing parent, left for spouse. Now Mameh's ribbon quivers against an old cotton dress, her translucent face partially covered by a plain blue kerchief, tears flowing freely. I edge nearer to wrap my arm around her. I realize I've already seen too much, come too close, as she shrugs her shoulders, moves away.

One year later we all gather at the cemetery for the monument unveiling. In the cool March air a white sheet flutters gently against granite as blessings are intoned. The veil lifted, Tateh's name is etched deeply, his life reduced to two numbers, the starkness of it final, reminding me of the thump of dirt hitting coffin as we passed the shovel one to the other. Now, clutching Joe's hand, I feel a soft quiver deep within my gut. My baby moving. Another child he'll never know.

Tateh's Ring

It rested squarely on the middle finger of his right hand, a hefty gold ring made for a man wanting respect. I suppose he bought it in Germany after the war, when he was flush with black market money. He had regained his weight by then. The ring fit snugly around his thickened finger. It must have made him feel like a man again, all that gold, all that bulk.

It was elaborately decorated, etched in delicate lines curling over the edges and down the sides, then flowing back up towards the center where his name appeared in script, *Aaron* with two *A's*. I remember the glint of that ring when he worked in the butcher store, chopping, wrapping, and cutting meat. I remember the yellow of it, like the light in my room, that night he came in tears, his hands covering his face, after a particularly painful fight with my mother. I remember Mameh, retrieving it from his casket, holding it gently, like a fragile piece of crystal before slowly handing it to my brother who wears it still.

Old Friends

"Sara, take, take more," Mameh urges in Yiddish, piling chicken pieces onto her best friend's plate before helping herself to a smaller portion. Sara, taking a breath between non-stop chatting about her grandchildren, raises one perfectly manicured hand in protest. Crimson nails flash against her freckled skin.

"Enough!" She says.

Mameh backs off.

"At home your mother doesn't eat," Sara tells me, ignoring for the moment the fact that my mother has sat down beside her, "only here at your house."

Food is our language. Talk about the buying of it, the preparing of it and the consumption of it, and Mameh animates. Mention dinner at a restaurant and her eyes light, she sits straighter, wants to know who ordered what, and asks about the texture, flavor and portion size of a meal. When we greet each other on the phone, the first question, "Did you eat yet? " is followed by "So what did you have?" and the inevitable request for recipes I know she won't bother to prepare. This, and occasionally the state of her aging body, is the usual extent of conversation between us. All else we conduct in monosyllable.

The two old friends are visiting me for the weekend. Mameh and I have come to rely on Sara's constant flow of words to disguise the familiar silence between us.

They met in the Pietchkow forest, while both were hiding from the Nazis. Mameh was twenty-two, Sara, fifteen, enough of a difference in age to bar friendship at that time. After the war, children, they turned to each other. Their friendship weathered the cataclysmic upheavals of youth, to, now, the insults of old age. In my mother, an iron weight bears down, tightening her like a fist. Sara, her opposite, laughs easily, enjoys life, and often wears flaming red. The two women are inseparable. While living in Heidelberg after the war, it was the friends' custom to visit each other almost daily, as they do now in the Bronx.

Over coffee, the conversation turns to Tateh. I direct questions to Mameh who nods to Sara. Sara's family hailed from Glusk, the same village as Tateh and his family. As was common among the small Jewish community, families knew each other well. Her fingers curled around a blue china cup, Sara chuckles as she relates memories of Tateh, while my mother listens quietly.

Prankster

He was a troublemaker as a child and parents didn't want their children around him."

He enjoyed being a rebel, like his father, Jonah, a troublemaker.

Sara lists his antics.

"He stole pastries."

"He unhitched his neighbor's horses from wagons."

"He opened pens and whacked goat's behinds, watching them run free."

It's clear to me how Tateh disdained rules. All around him Jews lived by rules, government rules, religious rules, all meant to constrict him, to stifle his will. Rule breaking would serve him well.

He left school after the fifth grade to help his father, and learn the trade. Jonah was a patient teacher, he a clumsy but eager student. The shop, on the corner of a bustling market street on the main road to Lublin, the single non-kosher one owned by Jews, was frequented by Poles, stocky peasants who haggled over the price of ham and chuck. His own people avoided passing by, the shop, a scandal.

"Because it wasn't kosher?" I ask.

"Because they were open on *Shabbos*, Saturday."

At the store, I imagine he rushed past Jonah to wait on her, sometimes cutting a bit of extra loin or adding another thick lamb chop to her basket. One of the only Jews to frequent his shop, a baker's daughter, I see her beginning to linger, chatting with him about ordinary things, things they knew in common--the weather, that year's harvest, last night's street brawl. When they began to see each other outside of the shop, he knew it would lead to family strife.

"They called her Paula. She was smart, good-looking, the only child of a baker."

His parents disapproved because she was older.

But they were in love.

He married her anyway.

Revelation

The silence of the deep.

The silence of the tomb.

A conspiracy of silence.

Silent prayers.

Silent meditation.

So many forms and meanings of silence.

So many ways to fill empty space.

They were taken to Piasek, a ghetto," Mameh said in response to my questions about Tateh's first family. Nothing more.

"I don't know," her response to more questions.

I could not approach Tateh. We spoke little, certainly not of such things.

Those silences created space for dark imaginings, deepening over the course of a lifetime. I was poisoned by them. In wartime, starvation I reasoned surely sated by cannibalism. There was no lack of the dead to harvest. I imagined crowded trenches dug with spoons and hands, unwashed bodies lying clustered against each other for warmth. I could see skin blistered raw from cold and lice. I could smell the rank odor of fear. I imagined Tateh, driven by fear, abandoning his family. Leaving them to deportation. I thought him capable of leaving them to save himself.

This is how, for decades, I convinced myself he abandoned them:

He slaughtered animals.

As a guerrilla, he killed Germans.

He never spoke of his family.

Ever.

Even in his postwar testimony to the Warsaw Jewish Historical Institute.

I assumed he was ashamed of his actions.

He was prone to eyeball popping, red-faced, out-bursts.

The truth is I feared him.

I feared the *clack, clack* of long butcher knives sharpened on stone, feared his piercing shouts, the lash of his brown leather belt, his eruptions of rage.

I feared he'd abandon me.

I feared he loved me too fiercely, his love embracing me together with his two dead daughters. Suffocating.

I feared him capable of leaving me to the same fate as children whose bones were crushed in stifling cattle cars, whose heads were bashed against brick walls, who received the Nazi "pill," a single shot in the back of the neck.

I thought him capable of leaving his first family to save himself.

It took only a bit of sleuthing. Google, a meeting with a Holocaust scholar, his testimony. Why did I wait so long? We cast our parents in different ways depending on how we form our identity. Looking back I see that I needed to anchor my free-floating fears onto him, to give them a name and a purpose, Tateh. Seeing Tateh as capable of such betrayal allowed me to separate from him. To extricate myself from the stranglehold of his longing, for his daughters, for me as their living representative. To become my own self.

Here are the facts as I understand them now:

Tateh and his first family were settled in Lublin when the Germans bombed and then occupied in September of 1939. Humiliations and beatings became common, and everyone forcibly branded with a Star of David. Tateh and his family surely felt the Nazi stranglehold tightening as food grew scarce, living spaces overcrowded, and Jewish businesses abolished. They were surrounded daily by starvation, disease, death, and finally by barbed wire marking ghetto boundaries. Tateh, according to his testimony, continued to work as a butcher in spite of the prohibition against Jewish workers, a prohibition punishable by prison, even death. I have no idea how he managed this. Did the Nazi's make an exception of him? If true, he would have had the means to feed his family.

One night in March, the SS lit the main streets and surrounded the ghetto. I can imagine the cries of surprise and terror. Many, especially the elderly and sick, were shot on the spot. The following day fifteen hundred people were ordered deported to the Belzec concentration camp. Liquidation of the ghetto had begun. From then on fifteen hundred people were deported daily. One month before Tateh escaped the ghetto, one thousand Jews were deported to the Piasek ghetto, a way station to the Belzec camp, the children shot before reaching that destination. Were Tateh's family among them? I believe they were.

"They were taken to Piasek, a ghetto," Mameh said in response to my questions about his family. Nothing more.

Tateh managed to avoid deportation. Jewish workers, registered with a stamp on their identity cards, were exempt from deportation. Resourceful as he was, Tateh likely worked on approved jobs in addition to his butchering.

The final liquidation of the ghetto had been scheduled for October 24. Tateh fled to the forest on October 21. Without his family.

The first paragraph of his testimony reads in part: *Of the immediate family, parents, two sisters, wife and two children perished.* That is all. No more mention of family. I imagine he fled to the woods and locked his trauma away, sealed it for good and buried it in the ice and snow of that first winter.

For years I could easily see my father abandoning his family. Leaving them to deportation. His silence, to me, an expression of guilt. Guilt I see now perhaps not about having abandoned them, but of having survived.

Prankster

Sara and I speak regularly. With Tateh gone, and Sara eager to give voice to the past, she provides the near ancient earth and I dig. But how reliable is her memory? How much truth in her words?

> "He was rough."
> "Rough how?" I ask.
> "You know rough, like boys."
> "But how?"
> "Rough. I was afraid of him."
> "Why?"

This back and forth continues for some minutes until,

> "He pushed me."

One of the youngest in the forest, Sara at fifteen, possessed the grit to survive. Could one push from Tateh have made her fearful?

Another time I ask her to recall. In her late

eighties her memories tend to flow one onto another. Here she remains on point.

"He was a prankster."

"Do you remember the pranks?"

"Oh yeah. One time my mother made a sponge cake for the holidays, Passover, and she put it in front of the window. In the morning they went out and the cake wasn't there. They knew who did it. Your father, his cousin Shayah, his friend Duvid."

She goes on.

"My mother had beautiful jewelry and one day it was gone. They knew who took it, but they were afraid to say it."

Tateh and his pals.

And then the horses.

The family's mode of transportation.

Their winter entertainment.

Two horses, pulling a sleigh full of youngsters across a snow capped meadow.

One morning, dead on the ground.

No one turned them in.

No one accused them directly.

"Why?"

"People were afraid. If you said something they

would do it to you."

In the telling, Sara, at times with an amused chuckle, dismisses this as youngsters' mischief, typical of the time and place.

I choose for the moment to trust Sara's veracity, and temper shock with more measured thoughts. The son of a butcher and himself a butcher by trade, Tateh surely viewed animals as objects for use and consumption, rather than the soulful creatures and companions many think of now. In another time, another place his might have been the actions of a criminal, a juvenile delinquent at best. I prefer to think of his antics as preparation. Fierceness melded with mischief readied Tateh for his future. I cannot judge him just as I cannot place myself in the Poland of that era. I note his resolve, his willingness to shatter convention. These among the traits that drove him to escape the ghetto. Then, when compelled to steal in order to eat, to kill in order to live, he seized his advantage.

Flight

Although the war represented a portion of her life ever alive and churning within her, Mameh did her best to conceal it from me. *I don't remember,* her usual answer to questions. I add my imaginings to Mameh's story, which she told in enigmatic fragments over the years.

Their village, Mentow, barely a dot on the map, had been a stepping-stone on the road north to Lublin, ten kilometers away. It housed enough Jews to assemble the quorum necessary for prayer. They prayed in Mameh's home, where Zayde, her father, kept the Torah, the most hallowed of sacred objects.

A flourmill, located along the banks of a river, provided what little economy the town could muster. Zayde eked out a living selling what he could on Lublin market days: eggs, geese, odds-and-ends. Bubbe cooked and sold kosher food to observant Jewish travelers on the road to Lublin.

In the fall of 1942, the Germans posted an order. Mameh and her family, along with all the Jews in her village, were to pack their belongings and assemble in the Lublin ghetto. They all knew what that meant. They had heard the rumors. They knew about the deportations, the death factories, the ghetto liquidations. They had just days to decide, then prepare. Her parents summoned Mameh back from Lublin, where, while staying with relatives, she had been training to become a seamstress.

I can see Bubbe, tugging at the bottom of her kerchief, moving her head side-to-side, eyes wide, unblinking, a shudder electrifying her core.

There's Zayde, working his jaw, his massive silvery beard quivering slightly, his brow furrowed in thought, body taut, planning.

And Mameh looking from one to the other, folding her arms around herself, holding on, her young face gone gray as ash.

I imagine for Zayde, first a priority, to bury the Torah. Even before they transferred the heavy wooden armoire, the oak pendulum clock, and the brass *Shabbos* candlesticks next door for safekeeping. Even before they gathered their own belongings.

He summoned those few men who had not yet fled, to dig a grave. The Torah, a living entity in their eyes, when in disrepair or disuse was accorded burial, just like a human being. Caring for the Torah as essential to him as caring for his family. *I can't leave it for the goyim to desecrate*, he might have thought.

Lacking a proper shroud, Zayde removed the scrolls from their wooden posts, touching the fringe of his *tallis* to it for a final kiss, then tenderly wrapping parchment in a white pillowcase before carrying it to its final resting place. He would have time to gather the quorum necessary for *Kaddish*, the prayer for the dead. Was he thinking of Nussan, sealing his spirit in a grave shielded by the Torah? Who would shield Zayde and his family? God?

And Mameh, her young life about to be uprooted, possibly extinguished. Did she curse the Germans? Now she must trust her parents to protect her as they always had. How could she know then that one of them would not survive?

Mameh carried family photos in a cloth sack and the memory of her brother, Nussan.

Zayde carried ritual objects, his *tallis*, *tefillin*, and prayer book.

Bubbe carried a cooking pot, her prayer book, and the ring Zayde had given her. Each carried a bowl and spoon, and small items they might later use for trade or barter. And blankets. They would need blankets. They donned layer upon layer of clothes, yanked on sturdy boots.

Mameh, aged twenty-two, her parents, her surviving brother, Yitzchak, and his family, left behind their thatched roof home with its hearth, the family cow, horse and chickens. Mameh left her bicycle, and Yanka, her Polish friend and neighbor. She left behind her dreams of becoming a seamstress, and, nearly past marriageable age, the dream of a becoming a bride, of raising a family. Zayde left behind the Torah buried in his yard, and his youngest son's remains, those remains enshrouded in Lublin's rubble four years earlier when German bombs rained down.

Hearty country folk, they knew the Pietchkow woods surrounding their home. In them Bubbe and Mameh had gathered kindling, foraged for mushrooms. In them they thought they might have a chance.

Once in the forest they knew they would be facing two formidable enemies, the Nazis and the coming winter. Winter's snow cover would bring the inevitability of tracks and an increased danger of discovery. They would need to stay warm. They set about creating a shelter, a dugout, large enough for the seven of them, Mameh and her parents, Yitzchak and his wife Basha, and their two children. A smaller ditch would serve as a latrine.

I imagine they found a patch of ground beside a small rise cleared to the south, sheltered by a grove of pines to the north. A stream gurgled some forty feet away. They gathered large branches to cover the hole, to provide additional shelter and camouflage. Lacking proper tools, I can see how they dug. With spoons, with flat sharp rocks, with heavy sticks, with their hands. The ground, not yet frozen, yielded. Their fingers ripped into the earth, blackened nails tore into the ground. They dug in frenzy, desperate to complete the shelter. Sheets of dirt rained down around them.

This, the first of several dugouts to shelter them over the next two years.

Third Hanukkah Candle

Each year on the third night of Hanukkah, along with three candles on the menorah, I remember Mameh lighting a *yahrzeit* candle for her father. She did not know when Zayde died, only where, the Majdanek concentration camp. I knew the bones of Mameh's Hanukkah story, very little else of her time in the forest. I imagine her story. Here's how I hear Mameh now:

For Yitzchak, his wife and young children, along with Bubbe, Zayde and me, time bent and stretched endlessly. Moments felt like hours, hours became unbearable. Days we lay next to each other in our dugouts, closely packed, gathering what warmth we could. Cousins, aunts and uncles huddled in their own dugouts nearby. Little sticks of wood jammed into the earth smoldered to provide light. The smoke burned our eyes, ash floated everywhere. I can still taste the bitterness of ash.

At night the forest awakened to the bustle of families cooking, talking, singing. Fires lit up the night like sparkling fallen stars. At night we boiled not only food, but our clothes to kill the lice that tormented us. The evening's cooking smells reminded me we had survived another day, a small victory. And then, the day over, sleep, and my perpetual nightmares.

On the third night of Hanukkah, the third night without candles to commemorate, Zayde and Fetter Nussan, his brother, were praying Ma'ariv, the evening prayer. Both were wrapped in their tallit, bent over their prayer books, bits of ice clinging to their beards. Fetter Nussan, his feet frostbitten, had wrapped rags around his tattered boots. Swaying slightly, he could barely hold himself upright. He had been suffering the pain of it for days.

We did not yet know on that day a peasant in the village had stolen a pig. When questioned by the Polish police he blamed us in the forest. He was a peasant whom Bubbe knew, had approached for eggs. We did not yet know he had divulged our hiding place. Another peasant, Vladek, one friendly to us, overheard and ran into the forest to warn us. He was a young boy, maybe sixteen years old, not yet hardened by hatred like his elders. I can still see him loping through the snow, his cheeks the color of ripe cherries.

"The Germans are coming, they know where you are," he shouted, waving his arms.

I remember staring at the patches on his threadbare coat not quite absorbing what he had just said. I remember noticing the leafless winter silence of the forest. And then, the noise. I can't tell you how long it lasted, seconds, or minutes, or hours. Everyone shouting at once, scrambling to gather what belongings we could. I grabbed my sack of photographs, your Bubbe raced to fetch Zayde and Fetter

Nussan. When, after some minutes, she had not returned, Yitzchak ran for her. From their direction I heard a sharp, low, agonizing, cry. Then Yitzchak appeared out of the thicket, Bubbe in tow. She shuddered and put her hand to her face. When she removed it, I saw in that moment her face had taken on a mantle of frozenness. Her eyes read lifeless, her expression blank.

"Tateh refuses to come," Yitzchak said. "He won't leave Fetter Nussan."

Bubbe stared through us, an image of utter loneliness.

"Mameh, we have to run. NOW!"

The barking of the Germans in the distance and Yitzchak's shouting brought her back. We grabbed her hands and raced deeper into wood. When we had run far into the thick, we flung ourselves flat behind a copse and waited. Then we heard the distant shots, one right after the other. Two bullets. We thought at first both were killed on the spot. Later we saw. Twisted on the ground, still wrapped in his now deep crimson tallis, Fetter Nussan's blood pooled around him in the snow. He bore both bullets. One to his heart, the other to his head. And Zayde disappeared, carried off to live out his few remaining hours or days in Majdanek.

Unable to bury Fetter Nussan in the frozen ground, we chose an impenetrable spot overgrown with bush and saplings, wrapped him as best we could, and covered him with branches.

After that I stopped praying. I went through the motions, said the words, out of respect for Bubbe and Zayde's memory, but they were empty words, hollow prayers.

What Tateh Brought

At what point did she allow herself to waken to Tateh? Much later? Before?

Was it whole-hearted? Half-hearted? Tinged with guilt?

I can only imagine.

According to his testimony, written in Warsaw soon after the end of war, Tateh delivered stolen and bartered provisions to the forest families, surely Mameh's family among them. Bubbe might have accepted the bread, butter, potatoes, cheese and cabbage he offered, but she would have refused the meat. Even when it was chicken and not pig. Without a ritual slaughterer, forest life prohibited the luxury of preparing kosher meat.

I can see young Mameh helping Bubbe accept his offerings, and blush as she gathered them. Her looks unremarkable except for the paper-thin delicacy of her skin, the narrow planes of her nose, and the pull of her eyes. Such blue in the eyes of a Jewish woman, a blue so expansive that it might have made Tateh momentarily forget his past.

I imagine her surprise at the stirrings within her, ambushing her at odd moments; little flickers of light, tinglings of hope. *Even here, even now,* she might have thought, in the midst of the daily fear that consumed her. When he strode into view with his provision-laden rucksack, and touched his cap in greeting to her, she may have felt a warmth she thought had long faded into memory. And when he was gone did he still capture her thoughts? Did she picture his darkly handsome looks, his thick coat with its fitch collar, belt cinched tight around his waist, and rifle slung over one shoulder? And had she observed how he carried himself, with the arrogant certainty of someone who would survive? She might have allowed herself the luxury of believing the two of them would survive, together.

And We Lived to See It: Story of a Jewish Partisan

From the Jewish Historical Institute in Warsaw: *Grende, Aaron, file 310/110. Born in 1912 in the town of Glusk, near Lublin. Butcher. Five terms elementary school. Of the immediate family parents, two sisters, wife and two children perished.*

Tateh's voice. Spare. Enigmatic.

Reading the testimony he gave to the Institute in 1945, I hear whispered words, *This, Feigeh, is the way it was.* I hold eight pages translated from the original Yiddish. His deposition outlines his life in the forest, first as a ghetto escapee, later as a guerilla fighter, fully armed and battle savvy, planting mines, blowing up trains, killing Nazis.

These words, my link to Tateh's story, rupture decades of silence. A silence woven deep into the fabric of our family's character. With them I envision him in the forest. I see him within that expanse of fir and pine. I can smell the earth in the potatoes that nourished him, their skins crisping over his nightly fire, and the primal odors that fear and vengeance worked deep into his worn clothes. I can trace out the nubs of truth in his words and add my own imaginings.

I met in the forest my friend Yual Tenenbojm.

Light snow falls when Aaron spots Yual in the clearing. They had been separated during a peasant raid. He whistles a thin stream of air. Yual looks up. His gold tooth glints as he recognizes Aaron and exchanges greetings. Aaron drops his rucksack and grips his friend's arms, relishing that touch as proof of life between them. At times these last few weeks Aaron couldn't tell whether he was still alive. He knew he drank in air, that his legs moved one in front of the other. The ground seemed solid enough beneath him. But were they his legs? His lungs? He does not feel them. Hunger and fear drive him now.

They talk of teaming up. Yual, hails from Lodz, and though he's not as familiar as Aaron with these woods, Aaron is glad to have his company. He believes Yual's even temper will serve them both well. Aaron himself is quick tempered and impulsive. Yual, like Aaron, had endured the Lublin ghetto until the night before deportation. On that night, insulated by darkness, they ran.

Now brambles tear at their legs and thighs as they

make their way deeper into woods. They wade through thickets of nettles. Blackberry thorns pierce through thin cloth. They navigate through heavy brush, climbing over upended trees, ancient pine whose thickened roots and tendrils snake down towards the ground.

They say little.

Their eyes dart side to side, then behind. They watch the arch of a branch. They hear dogs barking in the distance. Traveling down-wind, they know German dogs track Jews, that Germans reward Poles for revealing hiding places. Mindful to avoid stepping on fallen twigs and branches, they tiptoe over fallen leaves, so the snap of twig or crunch of leaf would not give them away. They have come too far for that. Already on the run for a month, they hurry on.

Hundreds of Jews would stand on Cyrulnicza Street begging a few pennies so that they could buy a piece of turnip to survive. Up to five and six families lived in a single apartment. Mortality from typhoid fever was considerable.

In a thicket, amidst bare birch and brush, branches cobweb against a pewter sky. Tree trunks creaking in the November wind are the cries of ghosts. He doesn't allow himself to think about his wife and daughters, or his parents for that matter. He thinks about the Lublin ghetto, the starvation and disease. Its streets filled with the dead. Aaron stopped seeing them. He stepped over bodies in the streets. As though they were nothing more than trash.

Aaron and Yual ran into the Skyrzynice Forest as the final transports out of the ghetto loomed. Aaron had heard rumors about the destination of those transports for weeks, about the death camps. He was soon caught in the forest by peasants craving reward, then shackled and driven by cart to another ghetto, in Piasek.

For two weeks I stayed in the Piasek ghetto. On November 20, 1942 eight hundred Jews were assembled, divided into groups of seventy, stood on planks placed over a trench and shot. Not more than one bullet per person. Whether the person lived or not, he/she was thrown into the trench and buried. The ground trembled for three days.

A shadow hovers around the edges and creases of his mind. He fights to keep it at bay. But the images return. In the Piasek ghetto men, women, children. Old, young. It didn't matter. He sees mothers clutching children to their skirts, heads buried against fabric, averting their eyes. A final gift. He sees old men and women whispering the *Shema*, the prayer before death.

With so many, the executioners, hardened by liquor, soon wearied, or didn't care. Allotted one bullet per person, they began to aim haphazardly. Aaron heard the wounded were buried alongside the dead. He can still feel the ground convulsing.

*During the raid I managed to escape and I hid in a Jewish
cellar. I left in a dark night, because I could not stand it any longer.*

Aaron bribed a policeman for freedom with a
gold ring, hid in a damp Piasek cellar together with nine-
teen others. They heard the shots, felt the earth shifting.
He thought he would suffocate in that crowded cellar,
body packed against body with no air, no water, no light.
He imagined himself buried under ground. Unable to
move from the weight of it, he felt earth crammed deep
inside his throat, his nostrils plugged. After two days, he
ran into the night. To breathe, just to breathe. And now
he cannot stop thinking of the dead. His wife. His children. In Piasek.

*We both decided to dig a hiding space, fill it with potatoes,
and not budge from there. This we did, and we stayed there for an
entire month.*

Yual wants to link up with a larger group.

"With more people it will be easier to get guns,
food. We can raid the peasants," he says. They know of
others hiding in these woods, had seen small groups of
families huddled together. There were rumors too of
partisan groups, fierce bands of Jews and Russians.

"We'll be safer just the two of us for now. We'll
leave less trace. The families have no weapons either.
How will we raid without weapons? It'll be no good,"
Aaron argues.

Yual reluctantly agrees to find a spot and stay put.

Nights shimmer with frost. Ice particles reflected in moonlight glisten like shards of glass. Snow flurries and wind howling through trees herald storms to come.

Winter's snow cover would bring the inevitability of tracks and an increased danger of discovery. In winter, they would venture out only during a storm. They find a patch of ground beside a small rise cleared to the south, sheltered by a grove of pines to the north. A stream gurgles some forty feet away. In winter they would drink melted snow. But now they scoop clear water into cupped hands.

Soon the ground would be frozen solid. They must dig now. They gather large branches to cover the hole, to provide additional shelter and camouflage. The pit must be large enough to harbor them both, as well as the mounds of potatoes they had each scavenged from peasants' fields. A second, smaller hole would serve as a latrine.

Aaron clenches his jaw. Yual sucks in air. They brace their knees on firm ground and begin. They dig with spoons. They dig with flat sharp rocks. With heavy sticks. They dig with their hands. Aaron's fingers rip into the earth, his blackened nails tear into the ground. He digs in a frenzy, sheets of dirt raining around him. Aaron bites his lower lip as he digs, his body rocks with effort, his fingers and palms raw as he throws himself into the work.

They scatter earth around the perimeter and among trees, trampling it back into the ground with their shoes, and disguise it with branches and leaves. They work through most of the night and well into the next day. Rest. Dig. And finally on the third night it's done.

The woods, the war, dictate their routine. Pressed into the hole covered with boughs, they sleep fitfully, the dreamless sleep of vigilance, and awaken to the continuing nightmare of survival. Neither day nor night, sleep nor wakefulness holds clear demarcation. The boundaries are fluid. At times Aaron can't tell one from the other. Hunger becomes their alarm clock.

Aaron and Yual wait until thick of night to build their brief fire, inhale its warmth, eat roasted potatoes, then roll scavenged sunflower roots into makeshift cigarettes, spitting out larger stray pieces that cling to their tongues. Spitting out bitterness. Spitting out bits of fear. To calm themselves, they speak of their lives before. Aaron had been a butcher, Yual, a shoemaker. They talk about their work. They talk of meals conjured in their imaginations. Aaron recalls the sweet odor of *challah* baking on Fridays, the chewy density of *perogi* cooled on a summer's day by dollops of sour cream. Yual, a prolific storyteller, recounts Sholem Aleichem tales and Hassidic fables. Aaron, who had served in the Polish Army, boasts of his prowess with weaponry. They don't talk about their families.

Under shield of darkness, they scout the area guided by stars. One night Aaron discovers a group of ten Jews about two kilometers from their hiding place. As he had heard others do in the forest he calls out *amcha*, Hebrew for "people" a code identifying himself as a Jew. A bedraggled group of four young adults, an elderly couple and four children, stare miserably at him from underneath crude branch huts. The children bundled in tattered bits of fabric, the adults swathed in threadbare clothes as well. The old couple shuffles in rags wrapped around their feet, their dark eyes red rimmed. They move slowly. The children whimper. All bear the charred tint on skin and clothes from the soot of nightly fires. To Aaron they look like denizens of *gehenna*. He realizes he must look much the same, a spectre neither fully alive nor dead. Unrecognizable.

The days grow shorter. Cold sets in. Then snow. Aaron and Yual shiver beneath worn blankets. Huddle against each other for warmth. Lice torment them. Hunger rips at their bellies. They have been hearing dogs barking for several days now, their sharp yelps getting louder. The Germans are surely closing in.

One night a tabby cat wanders near their fire.

Two potatoes crackling on burning wood send sparks flashing then disappearing like shooting stars.

The cat, exploring the perimeter of the fire,

bends low into its haunches, tail long and low as well.

The dogs must have scared the cat into the forest, Aaron thinks, marveling at the sight of this emissary of a distant, civilized past.

He holds out his hand, murmurs to the cat in a soft voice. Yual tends the potatoes, turning them with care. He watches as the cat delicately sniffs Aaron's hand. Aaron pets it in long, soft strokes. The cat arches its rust colored back in pleasure, begins to purr, rubbing against Aaron's leg. Aaron picks up the cat, and holding it in the crook of his arm, whispers "soft kitty." Yual gently squeezes the potatoes, their scorched skin yielding to soft flesh inside.

"They're ready," he says.

In one swift movement Aaron flings the cat around, grabs it by the neck and twists.

"Tonight we'll eat meat."

During a raid the Germans caught ten Jews not far from us, and shot them.

The next morning they awaken to the sharp barking of dogs. With snow on the ground they must remain where they are. Those dogs could easily tear a man apart. They are close by. By the sound, Aaron figures just a kilometer or so away. He and Yual remove their tracks and camp traces, race into the hole, cover it, and crouch down.

Pine needles rustle in the breeze. Aaron holds

his breath. And waits. The barking stops, giving way to forest quiet. Seconds freeze into minutes. Then, bullets explode the silence of icy air. A hawk startles into flight. He counts each sharp crack, one, two, three. Ten bullets. Aaron thinks of the old couple shuffling through snow in their makeshift shoes. An eruption of blood pounds through his arms and legs. He trembles, a slight shaking at first giving way to great tremors shaking his torso. He can no longer keep his shadows at bay. And he weeps.

But our hiding place was then not discovered.

We decided to obtain weapons, come what may. We met in the woods a few acquaintances that still had some money, and for a tremendous sum we managed to buy from a peasant a rifle and two bullets.

Reading through his deposition I can see Tateh's evolution from a ghetto escapee, running from the Germans, into a hardened guerrilla fighter, in control of his arms and his men.

More Jews were appearing in the woods, and our group grew and grew. About a hundred people were now armed. We divided ourselves into smaller groups of about ten each, and I was the leader of my group…

Woe to the single German car that found itself on the roads controlled by our unit. Germans who sought wood in the forest were eliminated without pity…

Their numbers swelled, as did their cache of weapons.

We distributed food supplies to about three hundred Jews living in our forest and in the neighboring forests. Throughout the forest there were scattered dugout hiding places with small numbers of Jews, usually whole families, who lived their special way in the woods.

He and the other partisans combed the surrounding villages for food. That which farmers refused to give willingly, they took by force. I suspect Tateh began delivering provisions to Mameh's family regularly. He would have noted Bubbe's refusal to accept meat, perhaps incredulous that she worshipped a God who might fault her for eating whatever she could to survive. He would have noted Mameh, been struck by the sky blue of her eyes. At some point in the forest, they became a couple.

During the day people stayed in their dugouts, and at night they cooked outside, on open fires. At night we did not fear the Germans...

In the winter of 1943 we simultaneously celebrated two weddings...

We also arranged for medicines for the sick women. But since our living conditions were not so great, we sometimes placed the sick-for suitable remuneration, or sometimes with threats-at local peasants for recovery...

Wounded on two occasions, he recuperated with the aide of medicines procured by stealth and force.

Tateh describes a heavy weapons attack by "a few hundred" Germans that lasted five hours. Tateh's group fought with rifles, grenades and pistols against German mine-throwers, machine guns and grenades. Fifteen Germans fell. Two lads fell from Glusk, his village and two partisan women.

Later on:

A small group of Soviet partisans came to us and invited us to participate in a joint effort to derail several military echelons near Minkowice. I posted sentries at both ends of the rail sector, and rushed with eight friends to the rails to place a mine with a timing mechanism. We hid in a neighboring glade and watched at the designated time a long German echelon loaded with war material arrive, and be reduced after the explosion to a pile of metal and wood. With joy in our hearts we returned to our dear ones in the forest.

"After the war your father still wanted to kill Germans," Sara had once told me.

After reading his testimony, I can easily believe that, and wonder who or what restrained him.

This was not the Tateh I knew. Or was it? The Tateh I knew wielded his hands in rage, tore meat from bone. The Tateh I knew ran in terror from a teenager practicing his driving skills. The Tateh I knew, a man traumatized and transformed by his past, remains an enigma.

His *guerre de plume*, Adam.

And then, finally:

On July 8, 1944, in the forest, we heard loud noises of tanks, artillery, and gunfire. We noticed long columns of German soldiers moving west, and we realized that the Germans were retreating. We raided smaller groups, disarmed them, and heard from the Germans that the Soviets were near. And so we waited impatiently for the Red Army.

And we lived to see it...

Jubilation. I can see them hugging, dancing, howling. I can see the tears of joy. Then, tears of grief and remembrance. Of those who did not live, in Tateh's immediate family, both his parents, sister, wife, and two young daughters perished. Mameh lost her father, brother, uncles, aunts, and cousins.

Along with Tateh's rucksack and weapon, Mameh's photos and Bubbe's scorched pots, they carried out of the forest a ravenous beast, *Dee Melchomeh*, the War. That beast clung onto their backs throughout their journeys, from Poland to Germany to America, its jaws tearing through to their unseen parts.

If I could, I would have warned them. I would

have said, *look behind you, shake it off, leave it here deep in the woods, or it will consume us all.*

III

Afterwards

Homecoming

E merging from the forest what mixture of grief, joy and relief propelled them to straggle home after liberation? By this time, with Bubbe's reluctant approval, Mameh and Tateh had become inseparable. I can see them, a group of vacant-eyed apparitions, arriving first in Mentow, then Lublin.

"What you're still alive?" A less than welcoming greeting from Yanka's mother, their Mentow neighbor. A common response, the villagers feared returning Jews would reclaim property, or worse, exact revenge.

They moved to Lublin, where Tateh had lived before the war.

I know this from Sara, now in her late eighties. Sara hailed from Tateh's village, and, as a child, knew him as a roguish young man. She is my link to them now. Sara, Internet searches, and meetings with a Holocaust scholar are threads I use to weave cloth that may never comprise a textured whole.

Through the help of one of the relief organizations, or through subterfuge, Tateh opened a butcher store, and all tried to resume their lives. With a vital urge to rebuild, to create new family, survivors married quickly, my parents the first among them in the winter of 1946.

And then the killings.

Again.

Across Poland.

Jews murdered.

Because of blood libel. Because they were taken for Communists. Because they might reclaim property and kill Poles. Because. Just because. Between 1944 and 1946 one hundred and eighteen Jews murdered in Lublin alone. One report, *The Condition of the Jews in Liberated Poland* from the Archives of the Diaspora Research Institute, dated January 1945, stated of Lublin "not a week goes by in which the body of a Jewish murder victim is not found, shot, or stabbed by an unknown assailant."

For Mameh, Tateh, and others, trauma piled upon trauma.

"How did you cope?" I ask Sara.

"We were young," her simple response.

"Not all young people had that kind of strength," I say.

And after a pause, "We did what we had to do. And your father and my husband kept guns."

And then, on July 4, 1945, Kielce. A pogrom

erupted there, fueled by a lie buzzing in the air. A little Polish boy kidnapped by Jews. His blood stolen by them for ritual use. In the exploding violence scores were killed and mutilated, scores injured. A turning point. As a result Jews were allowed to leave Poland without visas or exit permits. And leave they did.

My parents, their friends and family, headed towards safety, American Occupied Germany. Heidelberg.

And there they settled. In Heidelberg Tateh began a new career.

Wedding Circa 1946

In Mameh's photo album survivors gather in celebration, pressed against one another around tables laden with food and liquor, candles glowing atop linen cloth. Smiling they confront the camera full force as if on a dare, not a shy face among them.

They're in a hurry.

To resume.

To replenish.

To fill the emptiness of a lost world.

There are no photos of my parents together on their wedding day, or of the festivities afterwards. Just one photo where Mameh sits on the windowsill of a cut stone house peering down to the street below, a wisp of a smile on her face. Behind her, lace curtains part to reveal nothing but darkness. A flowering plant rests beside her, its blossoms an array of abundance. Her dress, a simple short-sleeved frock, hand sewn from fabric likely provided by Tateh.

No one thinks to take a photo of the two of them,

to mark the occasion.

Mameh's family considers Tateh, a widower, unobservant of Judaism and a *treyf* butcher before the war, a questionable match. But he is resourceful, a trait they cannot ignore. He will protect her, like he protected them all in the forest, keep her clothed and fed. He will provide her with children, bring her back to life. Help her recover.

Carrying candles, the bride's brother and mother lead her to him, waiting underneath the marriage canopy. Absorbed in the moment, the couple cannot notice, just on the edge of consciousness, a dozing beast. The room is stifling. The small apartment crowded with the dead.

Heidelberg, A Beautiful Life: 1946-1951

How long before they could afford our flat with its glass French doors, gardens, and pond that so enchanted me? Constructed of small stones, about two feet high and perfectly round, swimming in it, outsized goldfish, shimmering in tones ranging from silver and coral to coal and coral. Watching them I longed to join in, to glide through water aimlessly, secure, in that compact world.

"We had a beautiful life in Heidelberg," Sara says.

With the Reichsmark worthless and goods scarce, a black market economy thrived.

And so did we.

"What were they dealing?" I ask Sara about Tateh, and his partner, her husband, Moishe.

"Cigarettes, with cigarettes you could buy anything. With cigarettes I paid for my gall bladder operation."

In fact cigarettes became commodity-money, used by everyone to buy and sell in Germany, from 1945 until 1948, when the Deutschmark began to bolster the economy.

"They had people who drove them around. My husband had a Mercedes-Benz."

"You had a girl who stayed with you. A nurse."

I remember several.

For a hungry populace, cigarettes, easily transported, standardized and divisible, bought food. At the time the Allies rationed less than a thousand calories per day. With cigarettes as money one could buy butter, eggs and meat from a farmer, sugar and other staples on the black and gray markets.

Once more Tateh ignored convention and relied on cunning to provide. I don't know precisely how he operated. He may have bartered for cigarettes from the American soldiers who imported one thousand tons per month. Plenty of tobacco money there.

Sara doesn't know the particulars.

"I never asked."

I never asked either; although it's now clear how my parents furnished the sterling flatware, candelabras, porcelain, and Czech cut crystal gracing our shelves.

Of Heidelberg I remember the earthy dark fragrance of fresh brewed coffee wafting down from a neighbor's flat on Haupstrasse, our street. I called her Frau Kaffe. Her coffee, scarce at the time, likely procured by Tateh.

I remember the Neckar River, just steps from our

flat, and tossing bits of bread to the milky white swans gliding on it, the pleasure I felt in feeding those graceful creatures.

I remember gingerbread houses with their red tiled roofs stacked at odd angles, the grand castle and mountains enveloping the town.

I remember snow.

And I remember Mameh prodding, *Ess! Ess*! Eat! Eat!

In photos my parents, both portly, appeared to be catching up on lost time, their girth claiming space that had been denied them, just as they filled up on the luxuries of apartment, car, plenty.

In Mameh's photo album they're in smiling groups, fifteen, twenty of them celebrating, squeezed next to each other around long lace covered tables laden with platters of food and bottles of alcohol. Page after page of them. Here they are vacationing in a Baden, a mountain looming in the background, perched on the rim of a pool, thick arms around each other like loving, happy family. I sense their deep connection to one another, both in the physical ease they seem to share, and in bittersweet words held just inside the flicker of their eyes, *we're alive.*

I turn a few pages and here are the women, also in groups, proudly posing, holding up their babies for the camera like hard won trophies. And here I am, maybe two or three, wearing a silky dress with Peter Pan collar and cuffs, clutching a plush toy, a schnauzer, and beside me a toy goat, knee tall. Yes, it does indeed look like a beautiful life. A bubble life, insulated from the outside reality of a broken down, hungry populace. Perhaps that was cause for celebration too.

In careening towards life, marriage, children, where did they store grief? Were they as amazed as I am at the changes a few short years wrought? From living like hunted animals to outliving the hunters?

In the end they didn't care to live among Germans, didn't care to hear neighbors bemoan *Der Fuhrer's* defeat, or whine about the prosperity they might have enjoyed had he succeeded.

"If you wouldn't be alive, I would have been a big man," Sara's neighbor told her one afternoon, while picking up little Hans, her son's playmate.

"If they had won the war, and I was dead, he would have been a big shot," she explains.

It must have been a difficult choice: Israel or America. My parents knew Israel would embrace them. There they might settle among their own kind, revel in a homeland. But it would be a harsh life. By 1948 Israel was at war with its Arab neighbors and they had had enough of strife. They would, all of them, surviving friends and family, eventually immigrate to America. In America they would be sheathed in the companionship of shared history, and together face the hurdles of learning a new language, navigating a strange culture and deciding how they would earn money. Tateh's great-aunt Frances, who had the foresight to sail to America well before the war, sponsored our family.

They would begin anew, carving out yet another iteration of their lives.

Heirlooms

Twenty people are gathered for one portrait, a holiday perhaps, or some other celebration. The two patriarchs, Zayde and Fetter Nussan, features covered by imposing beards, sit front row center, hands relaxed on laps. Surrounding them familiar faces, some resembling my uncle Yitzchak, others, my cousins. All unknown to me except one. Mameh stands smiling, about twenty years old, wearing a light summer dress. The sole survivor.

Mameh won't forget that fall day in 1943 when the order was posted charging the Jewish families of Mentow and surrounding villages to prepare for deportation. She and her family prepared instead to flee to the forest.

Now, she refuses to return to that place with me, her village, Mentow.

The hunched, toothless, babushka-clad woman nods when I tell her I'm the daughter of her childhood friend, invites me into the thatched roof cottage, ushers me to the center room. Among simple wooden furniture, a clock, brass face blackened with age.

"Your family left this with us when they disappeared into the woods," Janka says.

On my return home, I write a letter offering money.

Two months later the package from Poland arrives, clock, brass *Shabbos* candlesticks. Ours again.

No money exchanged, Janka knew we had already paid.

Relic

The death camp Majdanek, casually preserved as a museum of sorts, was built in urban Lublin, the streets surrounding it tree lined, alive with the gear, brake and horn of traffic, with pedestrian footfalls and the hum of voices, with cosmopolitan normalcy.

Squat watchtowers still guard the periphery of the camp like meaty wooden ogres. All around, the sharp thread of barbed wire twists and turns, an agony of line. The camp stands intact, as though the inhabitants made a hurried exit, the ovens still operable, the barracks stale with the stink of starvation, overcrowding and disease.

Majdanek, a word I've heard for years. My grandfather, aunts, uncles and cousins were slaughtered here. That word, no longer an abstract, is made solid and real by these barracks today.

Families picnic on the lawn. I stoop to pick up a feather, a blade of grass, a pebble, keepsakes. Yellow roses bloom along the crematorium entrance. Inside, oven doors are opened wide, exposing gaping emptness. I light three memorial candles, one for Zayde, one for Fetter Nussan, one for the nameless others, and, for some minutes, let myself sink under the weight of the silence of millions, under the weight of my own fear of this place.

In one barrack's corner are mounds of blackened shoes, a mountain of leather piled topsy-turvy. With no one in sight, I reach for a child's shoe, flattened as though depleted of breath, think of my half sisters murdered not far from here, pocket it, leave.

I wrap it in soft cloth; carry it close during the long trip home.

I've reclaimed something stolen, from my family, from me, from countless others.

One shoe. In its singularity a symbol to me of all that was lost.

In some odd way, it feels alive, this relic. I'd like to imbue it with true immortality, with life breath. I build a box, a plain pine box, glassed along one side. The child's shoe rests inside. A depleted scrap of black leather, it spans the length of my palm, its width as thin as my pinkie nail. Over time small bits crumble away, like the Holocaust itself, fading from history into memory. Sacred, it's neither a coffee table object, nor sculpture, nor found art. An object of exile, I'm not sure where it belongs.

I donate it to my synagogue's Hebrew school.

Let it be a teaching tool.

Ess, Ess

Here's how I feel it still, a memory that unravels all of a piece:

At mealtime *Dee Melchomeh* shakes itself awake and climbs onto the woman's back. Its claws fit smoothly onto the round of her shoulders. Two plumes of smoke curl upwards from its nostrils. The woman can't see it or the tongues of flame beginning to dart out of its mouth.

The woman sets her chin just so, as she grips the wooden spoon and stirs the milky cereal, willing bubbles to appear around its rim, a sign of readiness. She despises this time of morning, her muscles taut as she gears herself for what lies ahead. Her own breakfast dishes, emptied, are still on the table next to the chair she's prepared for the child. Plenty of time to tend to them later. The child sits on pillows, elbows just barely skimming the surface of the heavy oak table. Gerda, a small rag doll, yellow braids darkened from hours of play, black and red dirndl skirt beginning to fray, bobs back and forth in her chubby hand. She hums to herself, softly at first, then louder. She knows what's coming, begins to kick her heel against the table leg fast, and then faster still. She enjoys the feel of heel against hard edge of wood, the jolt of it. More than the feel, she likes thinking about it, her young mind swirling around wood, nothing but wood. The woman turns to look at her, grabs a kitchen towel and ties it around the child's neck.

"*Hehr auf!*" she commands.

The child stops. The woman sets a bowl of mushy cereal and a spoon alongside the child.

"*Ess,*" she says.

The child takes hold of the spoon, plunges it into the cereal and begins to form circles, small at first, then wide and wider still, like the circles made by stones she tosses into the goldfish pond outside.

"*Ess,*" the woman repeats.

The child, not hungry, is thinking about goldfish, eager to go and watch them dance just under the water's surface. She cocks her head to look at the woman.

"*Nein,*" she says.

The woman takes bowl in hand, scoops a mushy spoonful, aims it for the child's mouth, connects before the child knows what's happening, before she can resist. The child puffs her cheeks and rolls the mush around from one side of her mouth to the other, not wanting to swallow, not yet.

"*Schlingen upe!*" she says, ordering the child to

swallow. Eyes widening, she scoops another spoonful and pushes it against the child's locked lips.

She'll teach this one to refuse food. What does she know, this child born after the war, what does she know of a hunger so deep, so pure that nothing can sate it.

"*Ess!*" louder now.

The child's lips tighten into a thin line.

The woman's face contorts, reddens.

"*ESS!*"

The imperative of it drives her now, the child must eat, must have another layer of fat to protect her. How else to survive winters in the forest? Screaming at the child, her mouth twisted, she smacks her on the back. She smacks her hard. The child begins to cry, great, gasping sobs. The woman, seizing the opportunity, forces another spoonful into her open mouth. The child spits, gags, and vomits the little she ate. The woman is in another place, a black place. The child's sobbing drives her deeper into black. She scoops up the vomit with her spoon, with such force, the snap of spoon scraping on plate startles them both. The dead ones, they didn't have anything to eat other than what they foraged, or dug, or stole. But this one is alive, alive and ungrateful. What right has she? She shoves the spoon into the child's mouth. The girl cries louder, chokes on the bitter taste.

The woman grabs the knife next to her breakfast plate, points it inches from the girl's neck and screams,

"*Ess, odder ich vehl dir derhargenen.*" "Eat, or I'll kill you."

The child gazes past the woman to the window and outside. She sees a ladybug crawling on glass, six perfect circles on red, climbing up, seeking a way out. She looks back at the woman, hugs Gerda to her chest and opens her mouth.

Mameh Distributes Her Belongings

My brother and I divide a silver flatware set, green and red cut crystal vases, porcelain statuettes of ballerinas, and some amounts of guilt about owning these mementos at this stage in Mameh's life. One item I cherish above all is her brown leather photo album, lovingly put together, and filled with old images of her family and friends in her village, Mentow, taken before the war. Mameh carried these photos on her back, in a knapsack made of rags, throughout the war. They survived with her. When I was growing up and heard about the war, it was hard to imagine a time when members of my family led reasonably normal lives. Everything before 1939 was unreal and shrouded in mystery, everything after so large and painful that nothing could penetrate it. Now in my hands was proof of life "before." Yellowed photos reveal young men and women, their arms curled around each other, their faces bright with youth and laughter. They had names. Mameh and I look through the album together and she identifies each person and relationship.

They had lives. I could see that by the animation in their faces.

One photo of my mother, although evocative of time and place, reminds me how physically alike we are. It's a summer day. The corner of a white washed building stands in the background. A large oak tree, in resplendent leaf, dominates the frame, its branches arching outwards. Next to the tree my mother, about sixteen years old, holds on to her bicycle. Her long hair tied back simply frames a round face whose sharp features seem open to possibility, a face resembling mine at that age. Leaning forward as though about to mount the bicycle, she could be riding into the village to shop for her mother, or about to visit Bashya, her friend across town. Perhaps she will meet a boy for a picnic by the river. She is wearing a light print summer dress that gently drapes her rather full body. Looking directly at the camera and smiling shyly, in the full bloom of youth, her smile both reveals and masks her pleasure. This is my mother on the threshold of womanhood. In a few short years she will be hiding in the very same woods she frolicked in with her friends. What were her dreams, before she learned that she could not dream? Her desires, before survival was the only desire possible? What did she think of sex, before sex meant procreation and not pleasure, before procreation became an antidote to death, and death something to rage against?

Spawning Monsters

Mameh began living with monsters at an early age. The Yellow Rabbi haunted her as a child years before the war, years before the directives for transport to "Work Camps" sparked her flight into hiding from those other monsters, the Nazis. Today she can speak in a limited way about The Yellow Rabbi, a mythic being. I've never heard her speak directly about the Nazis. Perhaps they're one and the same to her. The terror Mameh must have felt spawned my own monsters, transmitted to me and propagated like some bizarre DNA mutation. These black-booted horrors live in my imagination still, spewing ungrounded fears and dreams of danger that cause me to awaken suddenly to the relief of consciousness. As a child, the imagined embrace of a fairy godmother tempered my hauntings, tempered my dread of *Dee Melchomeh*. I was luckier than Mameh.

The Yellow Rabbi

Mameh sits with us towards the back of the packed synagogue, shivering slightly. Sniffling against the air conditioners' chill, she pulls the black wool shawl I lent her taut around her bony shoulders. Her mouth is drawn down into a grimace, deepening the lines and grooves of her pale face. An old woman in black, her blue eyes and rouged lips offer hints of another time, before age and war left their mark. Her features are still finely chiseled, delicate even, within the tributaries of those lines. Today, Yom Kippur, the Day of Atonement, Joe and I flank her. While she half-heartedly mouths the tunes and prayers she has known for more than eight decades, she sits in the synagogue this fast day sighing deeply as though wishing she were elsewhere.

Her own parents formed their days around myriad religious rituals and proscriptions, and she was expected to follow suit absolutely, or face God's retribution. No one had ever explained to her exactly what that retribution was. To my mother, it must have come first in the form of *Der Geller Rebbe*.

They called him *Der Geller Rebbe*, The Yellow Rabbi, because of his mustard colored hair, his real name lost decades ago. A boarder in her family's home, he instructed the village children in the intricacies of Judaism. As was custom, the girls were taught just enough to recite daily prayers and to keep a proper Jewish home, while the boys concentrated on prayer, the Old Testament and Jewish law.

Mameh rarely offers information about herself, doling out bits of her life that recall for me storm-tossed branches scattered to the ground, lying fragile and dying, kindling for passers-by. My question about where she learned to read Hebrew prompts fragments of story about The Yellow Rabbi, a moniker she can't mouth without flaring her nostrils.

"He killed a child once," my mother says, repeating in Yiddish the rumor she and her brothers had believed wholeheartedly as children, "beating him so hard."

Her fear of God was nothing compared to her fear of The Yellow Rabbi, whose teaching methods often included a sudden smack on the back, or a 360-degree tweak of the ear.

"Every morning he'd examine my hands to see if I washed them properly. If he didn't like the way they looked that day, he hit me."

More mysteriously,

"He never wore underwear."

And then,

"One day when I was older, he returned to the village wearing fancy clothes. Everybody could see how expensive they were. No one knew where he got the money."

"Where do you think?" I ask.

She offers no conjectures.

I imagine he tutored the children of wealthy patrons until the elders no longer tolerated his disciplinary methods, or, perhaps with his limited skills and questionable character, partnered in some shady swindle.

Like The Yellow Rabbi's old clothes, Mameh's stories are full of holes, enigmatic gaps shrouded within a fog of silence. She offers one or two scattered pieces of memory, rarely more than a sentence or two that, like callused skin, seal details perhaps still too raw for her to bear.

"Fetter Nussan's feet were so frostbitten, he couldn't run from the Nazis. He was shot on the spot."

"Your Zayde was seized while in the middle of prayers."

"We buried your cousin using spoons."

"We never found my brother's body in the rubble."

And so on.

And to questions, her response always the same,

"I don't remember," or "I don't know."

Kindling.

The Yellow Rabbi, as God's emissary, surely drove her away from God. I imagine the rejection of her parents' God was complete by the time war had come and gone, an unprecedented form of rebellion in that pious household. After her family had been shattered by war, the little remaining faith she had must have extinguished.

Still, she preserves ritual, lights candles, attends synagogue.

"Habit," she would say.

I gaze at the faces around me and realize my mother is the oldest person in the room. I realize too that this could well be one of her last Yom Kippurs. Her health is not what it once was. I would like to grasp her hand, hold her tightly, melt against her but a wall surrounds her. She peers at the altar with an expression that seems to say,

"You Bastard!"

I watch the hard look on her face from my side of that wall and inch a bit closer.

She Never Has Learned Gentle

She never has learned gentle having heard of too many trains traveling to too many dark places.

The train slows, rumbling softly, then stops. All is black, quiet.

The empty car smells of straw, shit and leather.

She pulls her hand back, screams "You Stupid!" hits the cat, hard across his back, hates this cat the one she tried to grab a bit too fast, a bit too rough moments ago, to kiss, the one that just bit her hand, then tail held high, walked away.

In Mameh's House

She's lived in this house over forty years. Tateh died over twenty years ago, Yitzchak, soon after, Basha next, my cousins within months of each other, Benny first, a diabetic coma, Frances, the ravages of sclerodema.

I visit when I can.

A broom handle holds the oven door in place, pieces of linoleum jut up from the cracked floor so that a late night bathroom trip holds danger to health and bone. The dishwasher, a birthday present from me, is gone.

"I gave it away," she says, "for what do I need it?"

The iron no longer irons. The bed half empty for twenty years creaks, its springs hard reminders that sleep too holds no pleasure.

At breakfast she lays out warm bagels, Nova Scotia lox, one large whitefish cut in four, head and tail intact, milky eye staring at nothing.

"Watch out for the bones," she says.

One sliced tomato, one cucumber peeled and

halved, one sliced onion, cream, Swiss and muenster cheeses.

One Lipton tea bag for me.

Diluted instant coffee for her.

She takes half a plain bagel for herself.

"Eat," she says.

Kissed by a Dolphin

Mameh has a lead weight tied tightly around her soul. Remarkably that weight loosened a few years back on her eightieth birthday. My brother and I had arranged a trip to the Bahamas to celebrate. We booked rooms in a hotel and casino, where our mother could shop, gamble, eat or bask poolside and sip pink tropical drinks. Throughout, Mameh's lips remained in their usual taut downward twist. On our last day, her birthday, we arranged an outing that promised a swim with dolphins. Once we arrived at the site, we managed to coax Mameh into a pool where two playful dolphins frolicked.

"C'mon Mameh, it's not deep."

As she took a few tentative steps, a dolphin emerged, balanced on its tail and kissed her on the cheek. Mameh's lead weight detached in that instant. The biggest smile I have ever seen sparkled across her face. A photograph of the event rests on my mantelpiece and reminds me that when she is caught off guard by pleasure, with no time to avert it, Mameh accepts it with every inch of her body. The photo shows her to be submerged in the water, uncharacteristically at ease, the dolphin alongside.

Contagion of Silence

"What was your father like?" I ask.

It's a lilac scented spring morning. Sitting side by side on my deck we're overlooking a field of fresh growth.

"He was nice," she says

Pressing on.

"How about your mother?"

"She was good."

"Who taught you to cook?"

"I learned."

"Why not go to Florida with Sara?"

"I'm not a 'goer.' "

Like a fortress, I think.

How alike we are.

I build walls too then chip away at brick and mortar of memory, beyond space and time. My grandfather was nice, my grandmother good, my parents silent. What was his favorite time of day? How did he carry himself? What did she call her children? The answers shrouded in cloth, like the Passover *afikommen*, in pieces.

Apples and Vinegar

The oldest employee at eighty-seven, Mameh's been working the Loehmann's Department Store dressing room for twenty years, now earning eight dollars and thirty-five cents per hour. She rides two buses to get there, travels one hour each way, but no longer works nights. Recently she helped snatch a shoplifter, was rewarded a hundred dollars for her efforts.

"I didn't let Hitler get me. I'm going to be afraid of a shoplifter?" she asks.

A pristine Indian summer afternoon, we're driving to an orchard to pick apples.

"1939" she says out of nowhere, "September twelfth when my brother was killed. German bombs. All night we searched hospitals." Silence. A deep sigh. A groan. "We never found him."

We drive past trees resplendent in fall display. A blue heron rests on one leg alongside the beaver pond.

"These trees remind me of Poland, two whole

years we suffered in the woods. I don't know how we did it. We were young."

On a holiday visit to our home the dogs nuzzle her.

"You hungry?" she asks them.

She accompanies me to the pasture to grain and water the sheep.

"You hungry?" she asks Daffodil, the black sheep, coming for a scratch on the head.

At the co-op farm, the cows, soon to be slaughtered, are mooing loudly.

"You hungry?" she asks.

Later,

"Mameh, how about something to eat?"

"I'm not hungry," she says.

One Orange Squeeze It

Some weeks after the funeral, clearing out your apartment, I happen upon an appointment book on the faux mahogany shelf in the spare bedroom-its spine squeezed between clumps of bills, photo albums, and a biography of Marilyn Monroe. Thumbing through it, I search for clues, looking for penciled meetings with friends perhaps, work schedules, or upcoming doctor visits.

The size and thickness of a paperback novel, the book's black plastic cover long gone, its pages lie frayed and faded. In it, in lieu of appointment reminders, I find partial recipes. Each page bears the recipe's name, provenance and a list of ingredients. Nothing more.

On Friday, January 2, 1970 a sponge cake recipe. I would have been twenty-three years old, around the same age as you were when your family fled into the forest. The page bears the crinkled texture of ancient parchment. Brown spots at the bottom suggest coffee spills or cigarette burns, two habits you enjoyed. In your curlicued European hand and loopy English spelling, a stack of ingredients.

Sara Sponge Cake

9 eggs

1 cup sugar

3/4 cup of cake mel

1 orange squeeze it

1/2 lemon

1/4 cup potato starch

End of recipe, end of page. Ingredients float in space without anchor to instruction. Missing from the book are the "how-tos," the what-mixes-with-what-and-in-which-quantity-to-form-a-whole, necessary for each recipe's completion. If you did know how to put the ingredients together, you never taught me.

Missing between us, the "how to" of mother and daughter. The ingredients were there certainly, in the sticky dough that bound us one to the other, the blood we shared, our indisputable resemblance to one another. In you I saw reflected my own face and slender frame, our cheekbones carving hollow spaces, our bodies, all sharp angles, slicing the air around us. Our differences revealed in our eyes, yours a veil of ice blue, mine a nearsighted hazel brown.

Scanning the pages, I discover recipes by Sara, Anastasya, Yenta, Rachel, Rivka, and others: survivor friends, shopkeepers and acquaintances, immigrants all. They furnish recipes from "home," Eastern Poland, taught them by their own mothers. The recipe book now peopled with the living, with friends and family. I suspect they recapture a lost identity through their culinary traditions, furnish sustenance from familiar dishes.

You cooked expertly from memory, on holidays serving up *challah, gefilte* fish, *kreplach,* chicken soup, *kugel* and *babka,* these among your repertoire of traditional food. Always you served yourself least and last, a reminder that you could if necessary subsist on less, had less need.

Perhaps you valued these recorded recipes, mostly sweets and desserts, for their connection to the women. I imagine you nourished by these women's spirits through the sweets they offered, anticipating the fragrance of vanilla and orange, then sated by the gift of recipe from them.

Here on Friday, March 13, 1970, *Babka,* from *Jack's wife from the dairy.* Did you discuss *babka* while Jack's nameless wife cut a chunk of farmer cheese, weighed it on the boat of an old steel scale, then wrapped it in stiff white paper, while you nodded approvingly at the amount? Did the conversation end with *babka* or did you evoke "home," recalling the perfumed aroma of summer strawberries, the bright chatter of young friends on a bicycle trip, families lost to war?

Jack's wife from the dairy

Babka

1 stick margarine

1 tablespon crisco

2 tablespon sour cream

3 eggs

½ cup sugar

Vanila

3 cups flour

2 baking powder

Crums on top

After pages of partial recipes I'm reminded of the spaces within and between us. Only the basic amenities moved our brief conversations-stock greetings, inquiries into health, family news: never a topic that might carry the weight of emotion, the hint of vulnerability, or the gift of the personal.

Devoid of opinion, you preferred to adopt as your own whatever you most recently heard from others. Although decades past the forest dugouts of Eastern Poland, you persisted in hiding, in camouflaging your being. In restaurants you turned to me to order "whatever you're having." Knowing you wouldn't follow, I often ordered non-kosher shellfish, relishing the mild sadistic jolt of it. I wanted you to wake up, to be infused by your own self, your being. I wanted you to choose, to taste pleasure. Most of all, I wanted to know you. What were your preferences? What dreams did you have as a girl? What did you feel towards me? I realize now you still lived deep underground, barricaded in your own safe house, perhaps never having fully emerged from the forest.

On Thursday April 2, 1970, a recipe for *Mandel Brot* by *Goldi from the beach*. Was Goldi someone you met years ago one summer Sunday afternoon on the littered sands of Orchard Beach? Did she bring her *Mandel Brot* to trade for your chicken and peaches while the men played gin rummy and Getzel plucked melancholy tunes on the strings of a mandolin?

Mandel Brot
Goldi from the beach
3 eggs
1 cup oil
1 cup sugar
1 lemon grated in
3 teaspon bacing powder
3½ cup flour
1 cup nutz
Filing Coca margarine sugar Jem

Whenever we spoke on the phone we'd share our default greeting,

"How are you?"

"Fine, how are you?"

"Good."

"What do you have for dinner?"

"Honey mustard chicken," I'd say.

"What else?"

"Wild rice with caramelized onions."

"How do you make it?" you'd demand and listen quietly, occasionally asking a question ("do you mix it all together or cook the onions separately?") While annoyed by our conversation, at myself for not knowing how to reach you, I recited the recipe. I did not wish to give, to fill your spaces with my spirit, to nurture you. A cavity so deep, how could I fill it alone?

If I were cooking something more complicated, I'd lie.

"A big salad tonight," I'd say, and recite the simpler ingredients, eager to get off the phone and back to my kitchen. These conversations plumbed the slim depth of our relationship. We circled each other in shallow waters, keeping uneasy distance.

"What are you having?" I'd ask in return, knowing full well you and Sara would likely share a meal at McDonalds.

"I made chicken."

Always, you ended with "I love you."

"I love you," I'd echo, hungering for a different mother, my tone flat.

Having felt the pain of mortal hunger, real hunger, you stocked up on recipes, talked endlessly about food. "Did you eat yet?" you'd ask repeatedly inquiring not so much into the contents of my stomach as to the state of my vigor. In case we had to flee again. Was that it? Or did food represent your attempt to bridge a common language between us. A reaching towards me. And I couldn't forgive your distance, what I then viewed as emptiness. I know now it was the best you could offer.

Mameh died a few months shy of her ninetieth birthday. Shortly before her diagnosis, a supervisor sent her home from Loehmann's Department Store, where she still worked, and demanded she consult a doctor. Mameh had arrived jaundiced, her tawny skin an early indicator of pancreatic cancer, and, as was typical, neglected her symptom. At eighty-nine years old, that was to be her last day of work. She left after twenty-five years and didn't look back, ignoring decades of attachment to the "girls" she worked and gossiped with.

Mameh withered. Her skin turned ashen as the chemo thinned her blood. Her appetite gone, pounds melted away and her eyes read surrender. I arranged home health care and accompanied her to doctor's appointments. My brother and I took turns bringing groceries and whatever cheer we could muster.

Finally Mameh was admitted to hospice. For days she writhed in agony despite hourly morphine.

Speaking with each other, even then, we couldn't move beyond the superficial.

"How are you feeling today?" I'd ask.

"Fine," she'd moan, her pain escalating.

"More morphine," I'd insist on the half hour, unable to bear Mameh's grimaced moans, and calls for her own mother.

Mameh's dearest friend, Sara, visited one afternoon.

"Look Helen, I've made butterscotch pudding for you."

Although she had stopped eating days before, Mameh's eyes brightened.

She opened her mouth as Sara lifted the spoon.

Finding Voice

I hoist myself onto a small table perched against one corner wall, and, determined to slow my pounding heart, close my eyes, shut out the dim light, and begin to breathe; *inhale, one two three four; hold, two three four; exhale, two three four.* After several minutes I feel calm enough to face the group.

I'm in a darkened hallway outside the meeting area, where in a stark room nine Jews, ten Germans, a translator and two facilitators, sit in a circle waiting for me to tell my story. It's my turn to speak.

Here in Wannsee, Germany, each of us is a descendent of survivors or perpetrators of the Third Reich. It's the fifth day of seven we'll be here. We're here to talk, listen to each other, and to share stories. I'm here to demystify "the other," the evil German. I'm here to confront the past and lay demons to rest. Five days now, of sharing meals, listening and responding to stories, German and Jew, children of victims and of perpetrators, together.

I had heard about the organization *One by One* through a therapist friend, attended a presentation, and after several discussions and interviews with some of its members decided to travel to Berlin. Their mission appealed to me. I recall phrases such as: *challenge stereotypes of the other, and interrupt the intergenerational transmission of trauma, prejudice and group hatred.*

I arrived in Berlin determined to have neutral expectations and to remain as open as possible to what might unfold. I was not a writer then. A local paper, having heard of my trip, had asked me to write of the experience, marking the first time I consistently put thoughts to paper. I wrote as in a diary.

Sunday-My home for the next week, a house owned by the Protestant Evangelical Church, appears bright and calming with its simple lines surrounded this sunny day by winter's dormant gardens and courtyards. As this trip wants no frills or distractions, my room, sparsely furnished and ascetic, feels just right. The predominant color is white, white walls, white comforter on twin-size bed, white for purity, white for the blank canvas of this coming week. In the corner, a small three-drawer dresser, and hanging over my bed, the ubiquitous wooden cross, a reminder that I'm alien here.

The comforter reminds of me of the down comforter I had as a child in Heidelberg, its feathers fluffy light, enveloping me in soft warmth. 'Feigehle,' the name my parents called me in Germany,' little bird,' sleeping in her own nest.

We are to conduct our meetings in a villa across the street, also owned by the Church. The Director of the house tells me a Jewish family who 'went away' during the war had once owned the villa. This my first taste of a particular form of German silence.

I decide to take a walk and wander over to the forest near the villa. The trees, dense and still bare, become silent surrogates of lost relatives who accompany me. My experience becomes our experience, the spirits and mine. The Aryan faces, and guttural tones of German I hear startle me. I can't help but think of relatives hearing the same rough sounds, perhaps accompanied by prods and beatings, shouted as orders.

Monday-*On this second morning, a day of beginnings, I head out for an early morning run to clear my head and to relax. People don't seem particularly friendly. No one offers a 'Guten Morgan,' or meets my eyes. I'm suspicious of the older folks I pass on the street. I wonder where they were during the War. What did they see? Know? What secrets do they hold? Am I stereotyping? Being realistic? Paranoid? There are no easy truths here.*

Gathering in the villa for the first time, we are a diverse group, our generations spanning from a seventy-nine year-old German Jewish woman who lost family in Auschwitz, to a Berlin University student, the grandson of a Nazi responsible for the deaths of thousands. We're scheduled to meet as a large group daily from nine to twelve a.m., three to six p.m., and again from seven to eight-thirty p.m. In addition we are randomly assigned to smaller groups of four meeting daily.

We're told Jews are always the first to begin speaking, the

Germans holding back. The first person to tell her story, Rozette, a Dutch 'hidden child,' describes being raised by a Christian family, her own family murdered. Later, the Germans begin to speak, their stories familiar. Germans of my generation, often raised in silence about the war, were stunned to learn about the Holocaust as teen-agers or young adults. History lessons ended with the Weimer Republic, a common refrain. Many sensed something wrong as children. Some are exploring the consequences of learning about Nazi fathers and grandfathers, and mothers in the Hitler Youth. Some are older and confronting their own part in the Nazi machinery. Although moved by the stories, I sit stone still, barely breathing, vigilant for any signs of anti- or philo-Semitism.

__Tuesday-__Today, during my morning run, I pass an un-leashed dog. The dog doesn't alarm me as much as the owner's barking commands in German. I don't like it here.

Five stories today. Jew and German alike speak of being traumatized as children by war. I note common threads: the search for identity, parental silence then rage, feelings of isolation, exile, deadness. We have much in common.

Renate, an attractive middle-aged educator wearing a bright silk scarf, speaks last, her words flowing through the innocence of a child's memories.

'When I was eight, my father dressed me up to march with him in a parade. I was so proud of my red shiny boots, my crisp coat, but mostly, proud of my father, the highest ranking Nazi official in our village, so regal in his uniform. Looking back, I think he used me,' she says, tears beginning to well.

After liberation, children flung stones at her because her father was 'the biggest Nazi in the village,' and she was barely led to safety by an American soldier.

If I hate her father, must I hate her? I can't when I hear the child in her. Does it matter who suffered more? Is the stoning of a child on par with one child's murder, or the slaughter of one million children?

Horror does not discriminate here. Jew and German share its bitter taste. Gertrude, for instance, must find meaning for herself in the wake of her Nazi father's ingesting of rat poison. She never learned of his crimes. Debbie must reconcile her Jewish family's banishment from the German village they'd made home for generations.

At night I dream I'm on a blind date with a man named Hitler, a comedian who arrives with a bouquet of daisies. I've declawed the monster rendering it a harmless figure, a pseudo-Charlie Chaplin. He carries daisies, a delicate looking but sturdy wildflower, perhaps a token of friendship or peace. But who is the monster, this Hitler whom I've transformed? The Germans here, or the Holocaust residing within me?

Wednesday*-I awake nursing an earache. What I've heard over the last few days pains me. I abhor being in this land. Though demystified and defanged, I doubt the Germans in my group are typical. While each describes the silence in their homes, they themselves have questioned, searched, spoken up. Many are therapists or have been in therapy.*

What am I doing here?

Am I betraying my family?

Some part of me has always wished my family's war experiences belonged to a bizarre fantasy. One reason I'm here is to experience an immersion in reality.

This afternoon Gottfried, Renate's husband, a lanky silver-maned pastor, the son of a pastor, recounts his early years. Like most boys then, he belonged to the Hitler Youth. A November night, 1938, Krystallnacht, Night of Broken Glass, SA Stormtroopers and civilians ransacked and looted Jewish homes, shops, and synagogues. Gottfried was there.

Eyes moist, his voice catching he says 'I looted a battery from a Jewish shop. From then on I was altered, no longer the person I thought I was.'

My heart softens as I hear the guilt and shame he still bears.

Thursday-*This morning Frank, a University student wearing long blond hair and John Lennon style wire-rimmed eyeglasses, tells his story. Speaking haltingly, his words seem to fight for form and sound within competing emotions. He is the oldest son in an aristocratic family. Near tears at times, he describes his grandfather, a high-ranking Nazi official in the Ukraine, responsible for the slaughter of at least 5,000 people. I lean forward, glare at him when I hear the word Majdanek, the concentration camp that swallowed members of my family.*

'My grandfather had been in charge of receiving the belongings of Majdanek's victims, collected by SS officials under his

command,' Frank relates.

Did these include my grandfather's prayer shawl? My cousin's shoes? An aunt's watch? An uncle's gold teeth?

I wonder.

'My relatives died in Majdanek,' I say.

'I'm sorry,' Frank offers.

I don't want German apologies. I have no need to grant absolution.

'In my family, always silence,' he says.

After his grandfather's death, Frank learned of his crimes from a letter in his grandmother's possession titled 'Unimportant Things.'

His family housed Jewish belongings. Frank recalls among them, a gold necklace, a silver chalice. These were cryptically explained as being 'from Odessa.'

Frank shows a smiling photo of himself at about twelve or thirteen, leaning into his grandfather who holds him close.

'I reject him, that monster.'

Outraged, I'm in pain and frustrated in its expression. Where do I put it? Neither Frank nor anyone else in this room bears direct responsibility. Bound in a most horrible way, Frank and I share a mutual dilemma-his guilt about actions not his responsibility, and my frustration in lacking a direct target for my rage.

We need more time to talk. The week is almost over.

Friday-I'm in turmoil on my run this morning. It occurs to me that Germany, the land of my birth, is home too. I take an unfamiliar turn, become momentarily lost and disoriented, then *understand this as externalization of an inner truth.*

This afternoon Frank and I walk in what Berliners refer to as a 'park.' In reality, the park is an unadorned dense forest where trees and shrubs hug both sides of the paths willy-nilly. It's a sunless day and in the dim light of the thicket we wander from the path. The symbolism is not lost on me, as we become disoriented. The second time today I've strayed from the familiar. This time I'm not alone. I gasp as, without warning, three feral boars run in front of us. The strangeness of the untamed woods and animals adds to my unease.

Frank eventually finds the way out for us.

Walking towards the villa, we are careful as we tentatively get to know each other. To my surprise, Frank admits to having been afraid of me. Another parallel.

That evening I tell my story.

Tonight, in spite of my natural reticence I want to raise my voice in solidarity with these people who share my legacy. I've been buffered by the honesty, and the poignancy of stories I've already heard. Taking a seat inside, I scan the faces around the room; Milena, Rozette, Renate, Gottfried and others, their expressions receptive, kind. Sitting here, bearing witness, I particularly want the Germans to hear me.

'I grew up with ghosts,' I begin.

'The walls in my home were decorated with photos of murdered relatives, their wide-eyed, enigmatic expressions frozen in time, their souls objects of my imagination.

Some of the earliest words I remember hearing Melchome, Vald, Antesemmit; War, Woods, Anti-Semite.'

Reaching deep into memory I gather images and thoughts, pluck out words. Momentum builds as my words tumble after each other and flow into a smooth stream. I speak of my parents hiding in the Polish forest, of my father the partisan fighter. I recall their silences, their rages and fears, my shame of their accents and European ways.

I have a sense of power, speaking, finally, and confronting the Germans with their past. At the same time, having heard their stories, I feel an odd kinship in our shared history. These Germans, mostly of the generation following the war, experienced their own aftershocks.

When I finish telling my story, Gottfried approaches, thanking me, asking if I will accept a hug. I hesitate, see gentleness in his eyes, fold into his arms, taking comfort there.

Gertrude, her hair pulled into a bun, a silver cross dangling from her neck, draws near, bores into my eyes, nods knowingly, and kisses me on the cheek. Recoiling, I step back. We'd not exchanged words before. This woman doesn't know me. Haven't we abided by an unwritten rule about personal space? Is she looking for forgiveness? Is she philo-Semitic? Hug a Jew to compensate for the past? A moment ago I felt bound to all the Germans here. Now I'm not so sure.

Saturday*-On this last day, I have a sense of hope, a strange, unfamiliar feeling. I now view silence as an enemy, and a lack of dialogue as prelude to aggression. I think of the Jewish con-*

cept of 'Tikkun Olam,' the mandate to heal and repair the world.

This evening, while packing for tomorrow's flight I hear a knock on my door. It's Frank, who's come to say good-bye. As we take leave, he places a rose on my suitcase.

We hug. A hug as natural as one of two friends parting on separate journeys.

Idling in Obscurity

Just inside the door of Rabbi Kaplan's study hangs a charcoal drawing of three Hassidic rabbis clothed in caftans and fur hats. They're dancing, suspended in air, heads upturned, legs kicking out, arms outstretched in rhapsody. How simple it must be for them, to believe and to yield to a divine presence, to intertwine that belief with unbridled rapture.

A ram's horn sits curled on the Rabbi's desk, its piercing call reserved for High Holidays, a wail that fills the soul. In ancient times it summoned troops to battle or warned of danger, that wail I imagine filling the sky.

Divine rapture, battle, warning, together an odd assortment of cues this day. I'm meeting with the Rabbi to begin preparatory study for my Bat Mitzvah, more than forty years after I carved a likeness of Rodan on my Hebrew School desk. This Bat Mitzvah will mark my fiftieth birthday.

My belief in a divine presence has been tempered over the years by history. The God of my ancestors has become for me a God of abandonment, idling somewhere in cosmic obscurity. These days I prefer to consider an earthly divine that exists in nature and in sparks of humanity. But I'm pleased to be preparing for a ritual denied me as a child. Ritual and study are my links to Judaism, to what keeps it vital and alive for me. The ancient customs, liturgical words and music transport me back in time. Here I am huddling under Tateh's prayer shawl, enthralled by the soulful buzz of prayer. Further back, I stand with my grandfather and his mother and father before him, all the way back to fifteenth century Spain, my ancestors' home of origin, practicing the same customs, reciting the same words. In spite of history, of torrents of blood surging over and again, this link remains firmly rooted.

Today, as we begin study for my Bat Mitzvah, I notice the shoe I donated to the Hebrew School some years ago, the one from Majdanek, high on a shelf behind Rabbi Kaplan, its glass case clouded in dust.

I think of the child who owned this shoe, running in play, dancing in delight, walking to lessons, herded onto a cattle car.

"It hasn't been used recently," he tells me, "the teachers have been busy with other lessons and plans."

"I'd like it back," I say without hesitation, reaching for it.

I will guard it for now, this relic. A last witness.

Exile

In my dream I am the keeper of a tiny village entirely enclosed in a glass terrarium. Dank walls of rock outcroppings surround it. The villagers, each no bigger than my pinkie, pass their days farming the land, tending to mite-sized geese and chickens. Horses and cows that fit into my outstretched palm graze in meadows, drink from glinting streams. The dragon sleeps high on a shadowed ledge, scorching the air with the past.

The villagers are the last of their kind.

To keep them safe for now, I seal the lid.

Acknowledgements

For their invaluable patience and guidance I would like to thank Christine Erb, Alexandra Garbarini at Williams College, Christin Geall, Richard Hoffman, Barbara Hurd, Rachel Jenkins, Christina Johnson, Mike Landfair, Marcia Loy, Lynda Schor, John Scherber, Rosemary Starace, Nan Steinley, and Baron Wormser.

With gratitude too to the late Michelle Gillett and the late Susan Hartung, whose early readings were vital to the development of this book.

Thank you to the Jewish Historical Institute of Warsaw for permission to reprint a portion of my father's postwar testimony.